The Quest for Gold

The Quest for Gold

Andrew Fekete

Edited by Peter Fekete

LIVERPOOL UNIVERSITY PRESS

First published 2016 by
Liverpool University Press
4 Cambridge Street
Liverpool
L69 7ZU
UK

British Library Cataloguing-in-Publication data
A British Library CIP record is available

ISBN 978-1-78138-331-5 paperback

Typeset by Peter Fekete
Printed and bound by CPI Group (UK) Ltd, Croydon CR0 4YY

To Mother

CONTENTS

Preface

For people who lack visionary power, or whose visionary capacity is suppressed to the flicker of shadowy dreams, quickly forgotten, the ability of some subjects to see things is difficult to comprehend. Visions may also be dismissed as hallucinations of the mentally disturbed. So we push the visionary world into the background and devalue it. However, the power itself is well attested – William Blake, Emanuel Swedenborg and Elisabeth of Schönau are examples of those who decidedly had it. The attitude of ancient societies was very different from our own – for if the king dreamt of seven sleek and fat cows being eaten by seven ugly and gaunt ones, then it was of the utmost importance of find an interpreter who can tell the king what that dream meant.

Those who meditate know that visionary power emanates from the centre of consciousness known as the 'third eye' or pineal gland that is subjectively experienced as situated just behind the forehead, just above the eyebrows and in the middle. This centre is responsible for the generation of pure light that radiates in pulses throughout the crown of the head, and creates an illumination that can turn into vision. A slight experience of a pulse of waves of consciousness at that point is what most of us are aware of with regard to this gland. Extreme fatigue opens this chakra.

Andrew Fekete, of Hungarian extraction born in Britain, was a visionary and abstract expressionist artist who died in 1986, aged just 32. He led an exciting but emotionally turbulent life that was dedicated to art, being not only a painter but also poet and writer.

A practicing Jungian alchemist, Andrew Fekete painted in trances directly from dreams and intense visions. His landscapes explore an inner psychic realm that is populated with faces, forms and images, and express a heightened awareness of religious values.

This volume comprises writings by Andrew that tell the story of his personal voyage and communion with the 'gods'. They take the form of essays, poems, diary entries and a novella, but whatever the form taken the reader should be aware from the outset that the material is autobiographical in nature, and that this is the prime source of its interest.

The anthology commences with an autobiographical essay entitled *The Voyage into Night*, written by Andrew in March 1981 in which he looks back over his life during the year of 1980. Apparently a document announcing a successful start to an alchemical work that commences with the re-discovery of a power of vision – "the projection mechanism", which he claims he was born with – the core of the work is the description of several dreams and fantasies.

For anyone to write about themselves and their visions in such a way invites the charge of narcissism, and it is not with a view to endorsing Andrew's own interpretation of the success of this first stage of his quest that I present this work here. In other words, I invite the reader from the outset to read Andrew's work with, what might be called in alchemical terms, *a pinch of salt*.

Approached in this way, *The Voyage into Night* manifests itself as a work of power and of captivating vision; the reader quickly sees for himself that the narrator's self-disclosure involves more than the narrator is himself prepared at the time to acknowledge. This dialogue between Self and Ego lies at the heart of the work's interest to the reader.

In *The Voyage into Night* Andrew does not reveal that his state of mind has already gone beyond dreams and visions – for he had started to hallucinate. The most significant of his hallucinations is his encounter with the Buddha. Two visions and a dream of the Buddha are referred to in the diaries, and the central encounter with the Buddha forms the subject of the final chapter to his putative novella *The Quest for Gold*, which forms the apex of the whole work, and in part only exists in draft form in his diaries.

Thus *The Quest for Gold*, the second item in this anthology, is another autobiographical piece that should be read from the outset with a *pinch of salt*, and as a fascinating window into the mind of a visionary, one who is not the master of the alchemical work he has undertaken, but rather, and in his own assessment, its subject.

Andrew made only limited use of drugs. Furthermore, it is not the method by which one comes to a vision that is important, but the vision itself. Andrew's visions are of a different order: one cannot help being impressed with them. *He was a man who dreamt only big dreams.* The nearest parallel to Andrew's work I can think of is de Quincey's *Confessions of an English Opium Eater*, where it is the overwhelming power of the visions that impresses us, de Quincy making no bones about the fact that the visions were induced by his addiction to opium. It does not subtract one iota from the force of Coleridge's *Kubla Khan* that it was a description of an opium-induced dream, and could not be finished because he was interrupted by business before he could write it all down.

Andrew's method was to induce visions by means of

extreme fatigue. From his teenage years he developed the habit of working all night. Binge working is an occupational hazard of architects, who have to achieve impossible deadlines; Andrew studied architecture and when a student at The University of Liverpool intensified his habit of working in excessive bouts. He also developed the technique of projecting into ink-blots – the technique that Leonardo invented.

Andrew would work in binges lasting two days at least – more than 70 hours without sleep. After a long period of sleep deprivation, as is well attested in medical literature, the subject starts to have hallucinations. This was Andrew's principle method – how he *entered the gate* that divides the conscious from the subconscious mind, and made manifest the contents of the unconscious, which he then painted. The nature of the material presented here as a whole attests that the visions are no mere literary fantasies nor the effects of drug abuse.

Part three of this volume includes a number of extracts from Andrew's diaries written principally in 1982 around the time he was writing *The Quest for Gold*. These counter-balance the tendency in the 'public' works to imply that the quest is on course and that he will emerge victorious. It is difficult to see oneself as the all-conquering hero when material life is not progressing well and, furthermore, one's dreams tell you frankly otherwise.

In his poem *Punishment for the Transgressors* Andrew expresses in complex form his knowledge that he is going to die, his interpretation of that process as in the first instance one of cruel dismemberment at the hands of the gods, and his acknowledgement and confrontation with the interpretation that he himself puts upon this process, as one of divine retribution for straying too far and illegitimately into the realm of the gods.

The unconscious, the world of spirit, is represented in vision as feminine: it is Mother Nature or the Goddess. To enter into the unconscious – to see into it and make manifest its contents in visions – then – is to see the Goddess naked.

The myth in question is that of Actaeon and Diana; Actaeon, the hunter discovers Diana, the goddess, and sees her naked; as punishment he is turned into a stag, hounded by his own dogs and torn to shreds.

Andrew has discovered that he is Actaeon. He has entered into the world of spirit, seen the Goddess naked, and must now suffer the consequence: cruel martyrdom at the hands of the gods.

Religions talk of the dual aspect of the Goddess; the Goddess, the all-providing, all-nurturing fount of life, is also the Destroyer, the goddess of night, the avenger, the harpy, the treacherous sphinx. And the Goddess does not like those who "accidentally" stray into her domain. On the contrary that complex, the totality of life forces that comprise the unconscious, collectively destroys the transgressor who makes this illegitimate penetration.

To transgress in this way means that one is trapped by the 'fatal fascination of the self'. Even from the outset of his quest, even when the life-destroying forces that he has unleashed by his transgression by illegitimate means into the domain of spirit have not yet made their supremacy clear, Andrew is implicitly aware that he will not live. He quotes from Jung in *The Voyage into Night.*

"For if the libido gets stuck in the wonderland of this inner world, then for the upper world man is nothing but a shadow; he is already moribund or at least seriously ill." (Jung: Page 293, Chapter VI, *Symbols of Transformation*)

In *Punishment for the Transgressors* the image of transgression, which implies guilt, is initially deflected into an attack on the indifference of society to artists, where the gods guarding their sacred domains are identified with cultural forces. He refers to the distinction in the work of Nietzsche to the Apollonian and Dionysian – Apollo the god of reason and order, Dionysus the god of the irrational and chaos. He begins to lay blame for his impending martyrdom on the shoulders of society, whose worship of "acquisition" is projected onto the bland preference for "Apollonian order". The tone is one of muted anger, and he revels in the glorious self-image of the Promethean rebel, one who challenges the gods of material society and wins a heroic victory by taking consciousness back into the territory of the gods, for which he is punished for presumption.

At this stage of our cultural evolution, we have either dismissed the spirit world entirely, or have relegated it to the unconscious. But the projection of the spirit world onto the unconscious has many merits. Although for the time being it seems to legislate that the spirit world is purely subjective, dwelling in the unconscious of each and every man, even if that in-dwelling may be said to be "collective", it has the merit of firmly connecting the spirit world with introspection – the power to go within and into one's self. It seems that it is a good place to start, theoretically speaking, for it avoids the obvious trap that if, for example, one sees an angel, then that angel must necessarily exist in the same way rocks and stones exist. In the first case it is important to be aware that one has visions with the inner eye, and not with the two outer ones.

It is Andrew's technique that lays the foundation of the context in which *Punishment for the Transgressors* was written. That Andrew was *not the master* of the vision, because it was induced by fatigue, is of vast importance. From the outset, Andrew's approach to the spiritual world that we regard as residing in the unconscious, was fraught with danger – for it was a bargain in which Andrew gained access to the world of spirit but in return for a loss of control of the generated material. That bargain equates to self-sacrifice and martyrdom.

His knowledge of his impending death is conveyed indirectly, by writing in the third person, and distancing himself from the painful revelation, seeing it in a disembodied way as a process – not as if he were Actaeon, but as if he were a sympathetic observer witnessing the destruction of Actaeon, or as if hearing of it afterwards, a visitor to the shrine.

That distancing creates a tone of ironic detachment and understatement that is profoundly moving. *Punishment for the Transgressors* is a powerful lyric, a subjective poem on a monumental scale. For another poem on a related theme there is Keats' ode *To Autumn*; Keats also interprets – in *Ode on a Grecian Urn* – his impending death in terms of a sacrifice of life to art.

> "Beauty is truth, truth beauty, – that is all
> Ye know on earth, and all ye need to know."

Keats died from tuberculosis and Andrew from an Aids-related illness. It was a physical illness that in each case brought about premature death. Yet the illness is only the physical manifestation of a psychological truth, and both artists put a construction on their own lives; Keats – I have given my life for beauty; Andrew – I have given my life for spiritual vision.

Yet Andrew also consciously accepts responsibility for the projections – if he is dying then he is responsible for his own fate. This conscious awareness is further illustrated by extracts from his diaries that conclude the section that begins with the poem.

For, as he states, it is we ourselves who are guardians "of our own recesses and powers"; the torment is self-inflicted after all. Yet with Andrew the complexity of multiple narratives is immersed in the complexity of his self-dialogue; just who is it that is coming into this realisation? Is it Andrew, or, the voice of his transcendental Self writing and creating through the upper personality? This is the problem of what one is prepared to disclose to oneself about oneself. One knows and simultaneously one does not know, or one chooses not to know.

We should not complain of narcissism. Andrew will not give up at this juncture the projection mechanism that he has discovered and brought back to us; he has liberated the goddess and suffered imprisonment in her place.

To be Andrew is to be *this hero* and none other. Actaeon, Marsyas, Prometheus and Narcissus are all heroes – the founders of shrines and city states. To be a hero to the ancient wisdom was not to have won to settled, material ease. The hero of the Greeks was that man who descended into the Underworld, penetrated into the recesses of the chthonic spirit, and opened up that world to us; passing through the gate was what counted, not coming back. So it was with Andrew. It was his faith. He lived and died by it.

And Andrew is right about society and the cruel part it played in his tragedy. The callousness of society and its willful miscomprehension of the artist's adventure dismisses artists as failures and imposes upon them the cost of their art.

This volume opens relatively late in the story with *The Voyage into Night* and provides glimpses in the extracts from contemporaneous portions of his diary of the underlying psychodrama. But earlier extracts from his diary would reveal the painful adolescence that laid the foundation of the drama and the part that miscomprehending society played in it. For Andrew is a victim too. His straying into the domain of the gods was not quite the willful act of trespass that the gods in their desire to justify the act of killing would have us think – for he was invited in as well – enticed by the desire for self-healing. Related here is the image of the sensitive homosexual struggling to come to terms with his sexuality; the dangers at that time, or at any other, of 'coming out'.

The complexity of Andrew's drama is illustrated in the closing section of this volume that comprises extracts from an essay he wrote in answer to Jung called *Symbols of Creation and Destruction*. It was written in February and March 2005 and concludes with a description of the life of the painter Hugo van der Goes, and his mental breakdown – another implicit piece of self-analysis and a final and deep insight into the fate of Actaeon, written by Actaeon himself.

Peter Fekete
Budapest, August 2015

The Voyage into Night[1]

My point of departure during this particular phase of self-analysis has been a simple fragment of memory which remains with me from the earliest years of my childhood. A memory of inexplicable events which I count myself as lucky in having retained, for even in my most nihilistic moments of self-doubt they have persisted as something which could not be explained away or diminished. They are the germ of my doubts as to the validity and efficacy or our rationalistic overview. That may appear to put a rather high premium upon them, but that is their subjective value and importance to me as a starting point.

As an infant I used to welcome the night, for to me the darkness of my room opened up fantastic vistas of swirling and multicoloured forms. A kaleidoscope of whirling patterns filled the space around me as they rotated, pulsated and hovered about me. Some of them were geometrical constructions which exploded into space, rather like the patterns we now know from computer graphics. First one line would suggest itself and would then extend into another separate one. Their relationship towards each other would then set up a perspective system of their own into which other lines and shapes could then be inserted and related. Other lines

---

[1] *The Voyage into Night* is a retrospective essay, written by Andrew in March 1981, in which he looks back over his life during the year of 1980.

curved away from me into hyperbolic space, whilst other forms were more organic, resembling the globes, fins and biomorphic shapes of plankton. Or else strange and exotic animals and faces would populate the space. With the darkness came the movement of these colliding and expanding forms as they radiated throughout my voyage into the night. I did not experience any sensations of fear or puzzlement in witnessing them, but, on the contrary, one of delight; the feeling of being enveloped within a warm and luxuriant glow of energy. Yet in attempting to describe such experiences I am aware that I do so from the adult perspective of retrospective fantasy. I cannot penetrate the sensations and experiences which accompany a three year-old-child's visions and dreams. Nevertheless, I have always held nostalgically to these memories as a kind of prototype; as an experience of pure enjoyment.

Some months ago I moved back to live in the area in which much of my childhood had been spent and as these memories came back to me I decided to attempt an experiment. I tried to see whether or not I could re-experience these same visions. As a child I would simply look into the space about me and without conscious effort would observe these gyrating figures. The literal adult mind, however, looks into space and sees only space, or else in the dim light of the room it picks out the patterns of the wallpaper, the outline of the bookcase, the wardrobe, and the pictures on the wall. The experiment soon gives way to the latest preoccupation, as the mind freely associates around one's day at the office, the tax return, the latest electricity bill or just the unreasonableness of one's struggle for survival. Soon enough one finds oneself drifting off into sleep. Nevertheless, in this respect persistence brought about strange results. I found that by thinking not of the objects I saw, but of a conceptual mental space, in the way that one might recall the face of a friend, that visions could indeed come to me and that the forms I have described began to re-emerge.

In an important respect I am aided in this effort by the fact that as an artist I possess a keenly developed visual memory and also the ability to form mental images. If I wish to produce a painting or draw something from memory or imagination, I often have in mind an image which I then try to put down on paper, and with this, the ability to translate the image into a finished drawing or painting. The production of images or hallucinations is rather like drawing in one's mind's eye, except that one does not feel that they have been produced through the exercise of one's will, but that they arrive spontaneously. Indeed one can stare into space for a long time and see nothing, but just at the point at which one is about to abandon one's efforts, one witnesses a sudden explosion of activity. Lines darting about like trace elements on an electron microscope plate, a sudden burst of forms which may only last for a couple of minutes.

In the period from that time to the present I have experienced many more occurrences of this nature and have realised that they are susceptible to analysis and are not as inexplicable as they once seemed.

First of all, they are familiar to us from the descriptions of those who have taken LSD, and also from the dreams, visions and drawings of those who have lost their reality function; those who have become psychotic and who describe the form that their madness is taking. Such visions express a potentiation and the psychic energy which is being released within the individual is thus expressed by symbols which represent energy; by darting filaments, rays of light, particles of matter, or through the formation of patterns. Jung described these elements as depictions of pure libido, as denoting the fundamental charging within the individual, and as coinciding with the beginning of the individuation cycle.

Encountering these visions I was forced to realise the importance of these childhood memories as my work had until then been moving in the direction of attempting to depict this kind of "tripping" experience. Once I had become fully aware of this direction, however, my work started to take on a quite different character and began to explore avenues which I would not previously have considered. Hitherto, the analytical nature of my approach had been applied to the forms and the conventions I was drawing upon, whilst their underlying motivation was only grasped intuitively. I deliberately utilised the language of abstract, geometrical forms, derived from diagrams or constructions which I had previously worked upon and which remained very much within the mainstream of 20th century abstraction in their references. Intuition came into it in the sense of feeling that I was groping towards something, having a vague feeling that there may be a way of expressing something that has not been expressed before, allowing it to take shape in a concept as clichéd as a fourth spatial dimension: in the notion of paradoxical forms, in objects which can be read visually from two perspective viewpoints, whilst at the same time they occupy the same space within the visual field. This act of connection with my childhood experiences made me realise that the source of this process is of course unconscious and it made me embark upon further experiments in order to see whether or not I could progress beyond this point of intuitively groping forward and find myself in more definite territory, closer to the

4

source of my intuitions, for after all, if there is such a thing as an undiscovered dimension it is more than likely to be found within the realm of the mind, or the "undiscovered self". This of course makes what I was beginning to embark upon sound more deliberate than it was, for at the time I had scant idea as to what I was doing, nor as to the potential psychological dangers I was bringing upon myself. It was not an intellectual exercise, but came as a response to innumerable experiences which I felt required greater understanding and resolution. I have learnt sometimes the hard way that experiments with the psyche are dangerous only when unconscious contents emerge into consciousness and do not meet with comprehension, or meet with superficial interpretations.

Although I had already been greatly interested in the theory of psychoanalysis for some years and although I am not an intellectual romantic, I did not possess the knowledge that is required in order to avoid the risk of succumbing to delusional ideas, and if I have succeeded at length in doing so, it has been very much a case of "learning on the job", and sometimes in somewhat strained and chaotic circumstances. Unfortunately one generally receives virtually no authentic education when it comes to an experience of the psyche and because there are so many parallels between this material and that of popular occult and quasi-religious and mystic literature, there are only too many false connections that one can become drawn into, or else one can approach these matters with an ill-equipped naivety.

Thus I was regressing unconsciously onto my childhood fantasies and using these creatively as a source of inspiration for my drawings and paintings, and also to a lesser extent for my poetry. I came to realise that such work was the form that was being given to a wider psychological development in me, that I was drawing myself back to the polyvalence and the sensation of the existence of many possibilities as occurs in childhood, but also to its lack of differentiation and directedness.

Recognising the unconscious source of my ideas, I then stopped producing compositions as such and began instead to collect doodles and to keep a sheet of paper beside me whenever I was working on anything else; whilst, for example, doing whatever required conscious effort on my part during the normal run of a business day. Far from these being meaningless doodles, I found to my satisfaction that this "spilling over" of unconscious contents produced ideas more intricate and compositionally stimulating than the consciously elaborated work which preceded them. From this point onwards I used the doodles as the basis for my subsequent compositions which would then be meticulously executed, so that although they began life as doodles they would finish up as something one could call a work of art. I found that the drawings and paintings which emerged thus in this way possessed a greater intensity and dreamlike quality, and that they were almost surreal. They were "better" works of art. They were more complex, more charged with feeling and worked on different levels of meaning and interpretation. They were no longer simply abstract or intellectual compositions, but it became possible to give them specific titles and to talk about them descriptively and say that they were "about" something. Then as part of the process of working though a group of related compositions I found that I could dispense with the doodles altogether and work purely spontaneously, and even automatically, and that as I did so, new directions and techniques were all the time emerging. This particular period of activity culminated in an event which made a great impact upon me. It began a period in which I began to work from dreams and visions. The following was the dream which inaugurated this development.

I found myself floating around in a void in space, which at the same time I knew to be inside myself. It was not an inter-stellar space, but one of grey nothingness; an absence of space, an absence of light, an absence of form. Whereupon an old man, clad from head to toe in a flowing robe, appeared before me, comically walking around in this nothingness, placing his feet first here and then there with disregard for the fact that there was nothing there. Every footstep was a gesture by which the void was dissipated and by which space was formed. Beckoning to me he told me that he would initiate me into a great secret and grabbing me by the waist flew off with me in the direction of a pin prick of light, which was just discernible in the distance. This he told me was the continuum of eternal space and time and that the point of light represents a fraction of time in the history of the cosmos. From that point, he said, all space and time recedes backwards and forwards in eternity and that the progression which emanates from that point never comes to an end. As he lifted up his hand, all the space below and above me opened up. A shaft of space moving concurrently upwards and downwards with a torrential gushing and dissipation away into curved space. It never began and never ended.

"This my young friend is your cosmos and you inhabit but the merest grain of speck within it, and the speck you occupy is no more than the space you exist in within the vastness of the universe. This point of light represents the universe in an instant. The continuum represents it in eternity. But what you think of as the void, the greyness of the void which envelopes the thread of space and time, represents our world. The world of the spirit exists beyond all space, matter, energy and time. The realm of God."

Honesty must compel me to add that I was not particularly well at the time I had this dream and that I had just undergone an operation to have four impacted wisdom teeth removed, and as a consequence was doped up with antibiotics and pain killers. In spite of that I remained in considerable pain and set about the task of drawing up this dream in order to take my mind off my plight. I worked at it in a fairly mindless sort of way for about eight hours, diligently shading tones of grey, with the only compositional motif in the drawing being an even line running down the middle of it from top to bottom. The shading of light was graded from left to right as darkness to light. When I finished the drawing and looked at it I had something of a shock. The grey on either side of the dividing line was filled with figures of people from many periods of history. For a good few hours I happily hallucinated, seeing in the drawing medieval gargoyles, a reclining Buddha, Mayan princes, Renaissance courtiers and courtesans, and my favourite author of the time, Herman Hesse, smiling benignly at me. I was even more pleasantly surprised when no longer under the influence of drugs, I could still see these faces and show them to others who recognised them and who could point out to me other figures that I had not noticed myself. Either I was witnessing something inexplicable or was unconsciously producing these images and was giving them form through my automatic shading. Most clearly the figures were not deliberately drawn. They were not delineated with definite marks of the pencil in order to shape and outline them, but they appeared as though embedded within the texture of the shading itself in the way that if you look at the grains in a plank of wood you might accidentally find some kind of outline which looks as though it could be a representation of something. Moreover, each one of the figures is a portrait in a style appropriate to its subject and period, and they also convey definite personalities and sitters.

In the meantime I returned to my more conventional abstract work and placed this drawing aside, occasionally bringing it up as a kind of conversational piece or joke. My attitude towards it was rather like the attitude one has towards a dream one does not understand. It was forgotten or disavowed. Similarly, I have not attempted to interpret the dream which stimulated its production. I simply do not understand it, although it occurred admittedly at a time at which I was in a state of distress, and if so inspired, it could not have been more reassuring in its overall effect. At the beginning of 1980, however, I found myself turning my back on my abstract work completely and started producing paintings within a variety of styles and within a genre in which I had had no previous training: impressionist and symbolist landscapes which feature mountains and precipitous gorges. The most important aspect of the production of these paintings was that they burst upon me in a completely spontaneous way and over a very short period of time. Normally I am used to spending three or four weeks or as many months in laborious and painstaking effort in order to produce one finished painting. It therefore came as a surprise to be able to produce up to three quite detailed paintings in a single night, and then to be able to sustain that kind of output over a period of time. In order to work like this one has to be able to paint very quickly and one almost has to pour the paint onto the surface of the paper. Much of this, although not all of it, proceeded in quite a random fashion, and yet the effects produced were far from random and give every impression of careful deliberation showing specific scenes in different but quite definite styles, so that some are close to the impressionism of Monet, whilst others are closer to the work of Turner or Pissarro. I have since then continued with this approach and find that it suits me well.

Not being a full-time artist or a student any more I do not have the time to be able to devote myself to detailed work, and yet the creative outpouring which exists within me and which is generally frustrated demands an outlet, and this is one way in which that can be released. It is difficult to communicate the sensation of surprise and discovery I experience when working in this manner. I make it sound as though I am simply slapping paint about and am completely unconscious of what I am doing. This is not so. I find instead that I am employing a different kind of concentration which rather than working from a point of departure which has already been defined as an idea or composition consists in the attitude of asking myself what is coming out of the painting, what is being communicated or being suggested to me from the brush strokes and colours. Seldom do I confront an empty sheet of paper with a set idea, but occasionally with only an impression. At other times I have set out with a very definite picture, but work pretty unconsciously. Thus I find myself using a combination of different attitudes which all converge in one finished work. Or else if I become "stuck" and find that a composition is not coming out and is becoming laboured, I abandon my resistance to it and generally find that this gesture fortunately saves the day and brings the painting to a satisfactory conclusion. As with the drawing of the single line, many of the landscapes also contain their hidden figures, although as with the Rorschach test I find that what I see in them is not always what is seen by others.

If I describe the landscapes they do not sound particularly remarkable. In many ways they are conventional and almost beaux arts works, but the fact is that they represent an unfamiliar milieu for me and have no precedent within my earlier work. I have hitherto been an abstract artist and so, producing the landscapes was a startling experience for me. They required no preparation or study and it was as if they came from nowhere and were being dictated to me. I had the feeling of being painted through. Nevertheless, I have been a student of the history of art long enough to have a subliminal understanding and knowledge of artistic styles and techniques. I feel that somehow I was making use of this knowledge and this demonstrates to me in a pretty graphic way the potential power at our disposal when it comes to an opening up of channels of communication to the unconscious.

So often did the uterus-like form of a canyon overlooked by ranges of hills occur in these paintings that it became a kind of in-joke amongst friends, abounding as the paintings do in male and female phallic symbols. Egocentrically one may want to interpret this symbolic realm of the mountains as that of the spirit occupying Nietzschean heights or as indicative of the emergence of a differentiated consciousness, but as Goethe's Faust shows, the principle of ascendency and spiritual yearning can so easily be converted into its opposite, that of plumbing those regions of the psyche in which are constellated not just the archetypal patterns of creation, ascendancy and light, but also those of destruction and decay; regions in which the light is at its dimmest.

It was also from this period that I began to regularly note down and study my dreams and conduct experiments in the meditative technique of active imagination. I found that this process of forming mental pictures into a narrative, a sort of conscious dreaming, was not arrived at overnight, but occurred at certain critical moments as a useful illustration of the condition of my psyche. Indeed I have found this technique more useful than any other in the psychoanalytical canon. It indicated to me an overall dynamic and sense of direction to my life, from which it has been possible at times to form a kind of self-prognosis as to what that direction means and entails. It has also tended to coincide with synchronistic events and also with auguries arrived at as a result of my use of the I Ching. Thus although some of the events connected with this have been most uncomfortable there has been the feeling of things working together and their being amplified through such correspondences. The following example very much had that effect on me and it gave me a greater confidence in two different directions. First of all, I found the images contained in it more unequivocal than those in my dreams, and secondly, after working through the material I found that at last I could understand Jung's *Symbols of Transformation*, a work which had previously baffled me and with which I had had great difficulty:

"I am looking across a canyon and whilst standing on a ridge there is beside me the figure of a woman; fair-skinned, blonde-haired and dressed in a simple Grecian tunic. The wind blows through her hair and ruffles her clothes which billow about her body. On her wedding finger she wears a ring which catches my interest. Its motif takes the form of a cross into which is inserted four diamonds, one for each arm of the cross. At the centre of the cross there is a single pearl. Holding this ring up to the light she points in the direction of the hills in the distance and to a tower which stands at the top of one of them. I take this pointing out of a direction as a kind of command and descend into the valley, making my journey to the tower on the other side.

Arriving at the base of the tower I find sitting on the steps which lead to its entrance an old man who greets me and hands me a key and a walking staff. These I duly take from him. I turn the key in the lock, open the door and enter the tower. Everything inside is dark and my foothold is uncertain. I am glad to have a stick to lean upon and tap out my way on the stone flags like a blind man walking along a pavement. Now that I have entered the tower and am in its very belly, the motif which I had originally seen on the woman's ring, reappears as a kind of apparition some distance away from me. In the centre of the cross is contained a dull and glowing light which becomes brighter and larger as I walk towards it. I hesitate for a moment and then enter its glowing centre."

This fantasy expresses in an almost classic form the drama of rebirth described by *Jung* throughout *Symbols of Transformation*: " .... that frighteningly narrow "passage" which signals the new day." It is to this point that we can be drawn; to the very point at which one can go on descending into oneself in order to drown in the ocean of one's unconscious, or to the point at which one holds back and is reborn through the symbol of the mother, through the rock tower, the valley, the canyon, the womb in the earth, through symbols which act as the mother within one.

Here then the symbolism and intention behind the paintings becomes more obvious. They arose not merely as works of art which were arrived at in a rather strange way, but as signals of a psychic event which was occurring within me. The fantasy represents, through the language of symbols, the problems of my then level of psychological development, a regression onto the mother or in Freudian terms, it can be taken as a rendering of the Oedipus complex. The Freudian formula, however, lacks all intensity. It displaces onto a mythological figure the drama which occurs within the individual experientially, whereas encountering the symbolic aspect of the complex is an altogether different matter, because one communicates with it on several levels at once, and most importantly, on the emotional level. I feel that in this way one communicates with the complex on its level of formation and allows it to communicate back within its own terms. This granting of an autonomy to the complex arrests one's concentration and forces its acknowledgement in a way that is not obtainable through the rational terms of a conventional psychoanalytical profile. Thus the fantasy represents also a kind of psychodrama, a point at which the complex demands a resolution through the incest symbol of an entry into the tower or symbolic mother, in order to re-emerge into the light of day; the light of consciousness. The symbols within the fantasy, the mandala form of the ring with its connotations of totality, the presence of the anima and father and mother archetypes, and the active participation of myself in the narrative, point to a conjunction of the constituent elements within my psyche. Indeed, by stages as I worked through this and subsequent dreams, fantasies and experiences I began to feel liberated from fixations onto the past. Nevertheless, this fantasy presaged a period of self-immersion which persisted for quite some time; about six months in all, and indeed I felt this to be a very critical time, an impression which was amplified by a number of synchronistic events which had a profoundly disturbing effect on me. These occurred at a time in which I was extremely dissatisfied with the circumstances of my life, but in which I was projecting my own internal difficulties onto external causes. I had become somewhat complaisant towards my process of self-analysis and was fancying myself as something of an expert when it came to my own psyche, not to mention in relation to others.

I was seeking to define everything I was doing in relation to myself and wanted very much to embark upon some kind of "great" undertaking; to establish myself, for example, as an artist or as a writer. I was also in something of a hurry to do so, regretting very much the time I had spent on other things which were not related to some kind of overriding goal. Thus in many ways, as I tried to push myself in every direction at once in order to excel, I was overreaching myself. The more frantically I engaged in my efforts, the more I was being forced to concede that I was becoming lost in them and lost to myself, and as a result, all my fantasies and longings revolved around the theme of escape; from life in the city and from the vacuum I was coming to feel existing at the centre of my own life. It was at that point one hot August evening that I pulled in the reins and felt that I had nothing to lose in confronting my life and taking it out of the automatic gear that it had found itself in. Returning to the paintings and drawings I came to ask myself: "What did they really mean?" It was as if someone else had produced them and not the little entrepreneurial businessman and omnimath that I had in the meantime attempted to become. Two works in particular stood out.

In "The City of the Scream" I set out to draw from imagination an ancient and ruined city which exists in Afghanistan, at the moment at which it is being engulfed and blasted by the shifting sands of a desert. I had no mental picture of what I wanted to produce and worked only from the emotional associations that that place set up within me, together with the response I had towards the Soviet invasion of that country. I had the feeling that world events were taking upon themselves an insidious and diabolical twist and wanted to convey through the image of the scream my sense of foreboding and dismay. Working from left to right in the drawing I proceeded with the notion of sand swirling about and obliterating the forms of the city. Gradually from the textures of the shading, vague howling pits emerged, and then rocks and towers and a gateway which led into the heart of a mountainside. This formed the entrance to a citadel and shaped itself into a kind of black gaping maw of rock, with diseased cascades of debris pouring from its opening. On either side of it were two towers, one circular and uncapped, so that one is aware of its appearance as a kind of hollow vessel, rooted to the rock bed through a twisted umbilical and prevented from soaring upwards by a sharply edged ridge of rock above it, whilst the other was square-based and capped with a phallic Indian dome, thus giving it an upward reaching aspect which is further emphasised by the terraces of rock which rise from above

16

it. These two elements, one female and the other male in their symbolism, were sharply juxtaposed and contrasted through the Hadean gate which both links them together and separates them. From left to right then, forms ranged from the indefinite to the precise, from being engulfed, to standing out in defiance, bathed in a brilliant and as yet unextinguished light. In the distant mountains a bridge of rock as a spiritual motif, forms an echo to the gloomy portal of the citadel.

Apart from the obvious dualism of the composition and its marriage between and differentiation of masculine and feminine symbols and its division between precision and vagueness, light and dark, and hope and despair, it was another composition which virtually drew itself. In this case I literally felt as though I was the servant of another hand that was shaping the work which was forming itself out of the materials I was using. On another occasion this sensation was even more pronounced. On returning home one evening I was gripped with a feeling of intense excitement and agitation, a sensation that something extraordinary would happen. In a feverish state I brought out my oils and set about working a landscape. This scene with its blazing red sky, orange rainbows, ochre hills and sculptured shapes embedded in the rocks was more like a hallucinogenic trip than anything I had yet produced. I worked throughout the night on it in an effort to finish it in one sitting, but was interrupted in the middle of my work by a fellow resident in my building who came up to inform me that the elderly Polish gentleman who lived beneath me had died of a heart attack and that for two weeks his decomposing body had been lying there undetected. I realised then that my sudden burst of activity and departure into this landscape genre had also coincided with the time in which the old man had been lying alone in his room, and at that point lost my stomach for it and left this particular painting unfinished. Reconsidering these events I felt that in them was to be found some kind of key. After all, what did the last landscape depict? Was it merely a hallucinogenic experience which I had unearthed unconsciously, or was it an act of connection with another order of reality, going beyond the realm of my own personal unconscious? Interesting as though my experiences had been, they were not something that could force me into a deeper analysis of myself, for they retained that element of gratuitous stimulation and excitement; the sensation of being a spectator rather than a participant. Thus the feeling that one is witnessing something remarkable or experiencing something new mitigates against an understanding of it as a psychic occurrence within one and leads one to lose sight of the relationship one has with it. Nevertheless, on that August evening I found myself opening up once more to the whole question of my relationship to such experiences. I felt it was a matter of remaining sensitive to them for a sufficiently long period of time, riding with them and not allowing myself a "cut-off' point or escape from them, avoiding the desire to turn back and find safer ground.

Such thoughts reeled through my mind as I raced home, uncertain of how I could shape my own individual response to them, for above all, I was also feeling that obligation within myself to make a commitment of some kind, as definite a contribution as I could make, towards the collective task of pouring contents into the vacuum. And for the first time I felt vulnerable and less street-wise and observed about me anxious and greedy faces, or just the faces of those with nothing to gain or lose, feeling and perceiving my own separateness and admitting to my eccentricity as a follower of fashion, stepping in and out of taxies, returning from and going to parties and nightclubs in the West End, rubbing shoulders with the famous, and whilst living, ironically, on the edge of one of the poorest ghettos in the city. I felt, without exaggerating it, as one of an endangered species. On three occasions during that journey I felt a distinct premonition or foreboding. The little voice which says, "Turn around and go another way", and each time I ignored it, let it get a little louder. I persuaded myself that such fears were irrational and that these were my streets as well. Streets in which I had jostled and joked with the black kids of the neighbourhood, streets I had ambled along on my way to work or to the shops, merging with the ebb and flow of people coming and going from the two stations, the taxi ranks and the buses.

The walk from the station is not exactly the most pleasant of ones. Derelict land. The row of station shops wedged into a tight island. The garage selling secondhand cars, the construction site for the new main line sewer, and the long and high wall to the station. People walk through here in a hurry, naturally clinging to that wall. It's a place to get through and out of. A paranoid's dream which culminates in a rough and seedy venue, the Bedford Hotel, outside which the local thugs gather in search of trouble or trade. Crossing the road and passing by that place I sensed their brand of entertainment and knew it was coming my way. Easing my breathing and relaxing for a moment, I slipped on some dog shit. It's supposed to be lucky.

The scene which followed was the classic one. Surrounded by a gang of six youths. Pinned against the railings and playing for time with conversation to humour them. Taking the punches, hitting the ground and bouncing up fast to make it for the break. Running for all my might and thankful for my dance training and the jogging I had done throughout the summer. Honour intact, wallet and credit cards still in my possession. Of course, afterwards you go to pieces. You notice the tears in your clothes, the blood on your hands where you fell, the ache in the groin where you were kicked, but it could have been much worse. In the aftermath comes the shock. The paranoia of passing the spot in which you were attacked and the absurdity of seeing assailants in anyone who comes near you. Still, you recover.

On the next late night venture home I decided to avoid all that fear, unnecessary fear, which you cope with when you've recovered from your injuries. You leave it until then. Let's go through the middle class district. It's safe. You know nothing ever happens there. The smart contained houses, the apartment blocks and restaurants. That's what it comes down to, knowing that you are safe with your own people.   Getting off the bus and crossing the road I noticed a crowd of people gathered in a silent huddle around a man lying on the ground, motionless and quite dead. Policemen were taping off the pavement and setting up an "incident room". By the next day only the sanitising white tape reminds you of the scene of the murder. Broken glass through the jugular vein. Out on the night before his wedding the man had stepped in to stop a fight. Across the road, his girlfriend had witnessed the scene from her apartment. Her hairdressing salon, but a few doors away, remains closed for the following weeks. This is too close. We're no longer in the ghetto. It's right here, where I live.

Witnessing that scene shook me up completely. It put what happened to me into its place. A petty incident when compared with this tragedy. So I planned to go around in taxies for a few days until I'd recovered from my escalating paranoia and until I could walk about without looking behind me. Therefore, the next night I jumped into a cab after delaying my departure for home with a few drinks at my favourite nightclub. So the taxi driver robs me. The next day the flat is broken into and every penny is stolen. It gets closer. They even urinated on the kitchen floor.

Forget it. You don't live like that in total fear. You walk the streets and start enjoying yourself again. So getting home the following night I relaxed into a bottle of scotch and started playing around with the I Ching. Why is everything red? I'm writing into a little red book with a red pen, wearing a red jumper and now the pain. My insides feel as though they are falling apart. I feel strange, really strange. Groping around I feel a blood clot the size of a sixpence and in my imagination feel blood oozing from it. What is this trip I'm laying on myself? I lie down. I can't stand it.

"I am floating through a beautiful meadow. I can see it mentally. It's not a vision or some kind of hallucination. I see it somewhere else. It's in my head. I'm looking around the room at the same time. It was no good painting that wall cameo, since there's too much pink in it. If I get the chance, I'll paint it white. I can live with that wall if it's white, but cameo is too dull. The grass is shimmering in the wind; currents of green in movement, and dotted about in it, thousands of bright pinpoints of colour. Tiny flowers. At the edge of the meadow, deep green foliage. It is so dense it absorbs light, and behind this layer, another layer of even darker trees. It's like the edge of a Siberian forest. It's almost black. At the point of connection between the trees and the sky, and the trees and the foliage, and the foliage and the grass, each layer gives off an aura. The tops of the trees dissolve into light, and the sky is so blue it pierces. Not a cloud in sight. A sharp primary blue.

Lying down in a barge, some kind hand has placed a blanket over me. One of those old fashioned tartan ones. I'm enjoying the gentle gliding along the water, the silent movement down the canal. The banks are steeply steeped up at 45 degree angles; deliberately cut and landscaped. Cypresses are planted in neat rows along the banks. The sunset bathes the water with a turbulent cataract of red. Who is it behind me? I cannot move. I cannot turn my head.

Floating. Rising. It's all in my control. I can go on rising out of myself until I've left. This is not the time.

Lying on my bed, close to sleep I hear for the first time the storm raging outside my window. Opening the blind I see the trees in violent movement. It's a wing dingers, but I hadn't heard the storm."

Certainly, given my preoccupations at the time, this was something of a purgative trip. It is also one which takes the earlier rebirth symbolism in my rock tower fantasy, one stage further. The coincidence between my thoughts and the events I had experienced was uncanny and shocked me rigid, for one of the things which had really been preying upon my mind had been the relentless drift into violence which is occurring in British society and

London in particular. Indeed I was shocked as a result of my panic in discovering my little blood clot into an out of the body experience. Either my thoughts were being projected and were creating the situations in which I could become attacked, in which I would witness the scene of a murder and would be robbed in my own home, or else the events and I were being connected up in some way. To accept the first proposition means accepting one of the principles of magic, whereby things are invoked or conjured up and made to happen through the exercise of one's will and through desiring them to happen. Or else one is unconsciously seeking out and being drawn into situations one has previously been considering only as a hypothesis; here, the abstract question of violence and evil.

One thereby invokes and conjures up what one is looking for in the first place and the magic works simply on the level of illusion. That is, in finding the thing you know you will find and through being drawn to it almost magnetically. Accepting that brings you face-to-face with the issue of unconscious motivation. Ordinarily one would not want to get involved in situations like that, and so what is one to make of an unconscious desire to involve oneself in disasters? At the same time, how is it then that unconsciously one can sense and divine these occurrences and be drawn to them? Is it simply chance? Is the victim of the murder or the attack simply a passive element falling accidentally prey to another's murderous or destructive impulses, or does he or she give some kind of bizarre compliance in advance?

When considering these events it is also tempting to think in terms of portents and communications from "another world". For example, one of the most arresting synchronistic events I have experienced happened late one night when I was fantasising about how best one should attempt to escape in the event of a nuclear holocaust. I allowed myself to doodle house designs for a mountain retreat, a veritable Nietszchean eerie, I would build for myself in the safe haven of New Zealand. I had just finished one drawing I was particularly satisfied with for an abode which was a combination of Classical temple and cave, when the telephone rang. On the other end came the pips of a long distance connection. It turned out to be a wrong number, but the person at the other end was a telephone operator in Auckland. So I could take the telephone call from New Zealand as a kind of confirmation of the coming of the holocaust or as a seal of approval for my fantasy design in that connection; rather delusional interpretations to be sure.

"For if the libido gets stuck in the wonderland of this inner world, then for the upper world man is nothing but a shadow; he is already moribund or at least seriously ill" (Jung: Page 293, Chapter VI, *Symbols of Transformation*)

The more one experiences synchronistic events the more one can get confused in the face of the contradiction between the causality of one's everyday life and the exceptions to that rule. The more regular one's experience of these exceptions the more one's view has to change in order to avoid the confusion, the apparent non-equatability involved in the contradiction. With the synchronistic connection, in the sense that events group themselves into series or form themselves into implausible coincidences, the causal limitations that apply to the empirical reality we construct appear no longer to operate. It seems that they occur in conjunction with the act of reconnection between the conscious mind and the unconscious.

Without the ability to differentiate between the fantasies and the empirical reality one can feel as though the fantasies are in hot pursuit and as though the world is "out to get one", unable to localise the paranoia as an internal event. The next escalation in the drama could well be the unfortunate one of stepping under a bus or a train, for the murderous impulses can also occur within one and can be directed against oneself. We can give ourselves over to the darkness within one or the tendency to go on venturing into oneself in order not to return.

The following dream represents just this sort of situation and also something of a crisis. On having it I was extremely disturbed by it. Not in the sense of my feeling that it was a nightmare, but I felt that something critical had happened in it.

"A beautiful woman has been imprisoned in a castle. We do not know what her particular crime is, but she is not alone and has an accomplice, perhaps also on some secret mission. She is blonde, busty, curvaceous and sexy. Teetering on ridiculously high heels, but hardly defenceless and weak. Rather, she is using her femininity as a mask or weapon to confuse and ensnare the men around her.

Having resolved to escape her prison, she distracts the guard and fells him most effectively with a karate chop. The noise of his weapons hitting the stone steps is such, however, that it arouses the attention of the other guards, the castle's sheriff and myself as we make our tour of duty.

With stealthy cat-like movements our villainess returns to her cell and locks herself in, having secured the keys to the room before being so hasty as to raise the alarm to her own escape attempt. Climbing up onto the window ledge she produces from amongst the folds of her clothing a good length of rope and securely attaches this to the bars and begins her descent at the moment at which we burst through into her cell.

Expressing his frustration at the successful escape, the sheriff begins to shoot arrows at the rope and succeeds in breaking several of its chords. At this point, not wishing to be party to murder, I intercede vehemently and suggest hauling our friend back up and capturing her alive rather than allowing her to drop to a certain death on the rocks below. However, at the moment at which I grasp the rope, the last chords break and at this timely juncture she lies completely in my power. Her life is literally in my hands and dangles thus by a thread. Whilst shouting back to my colleague that I have her trapped I slowly ease away the rope and let her down. "Now jump and run," I shout to her. Landing on her feet she hesitates for a moment, standing upon the castle's podium, as charwomen from the village are washing the steps unperturbed by this escapade. Whereupon she turns on her heels and runs."

All in all, the more I have set out to examine my dreams and open up myself to the world of the unconscious, the more I have had to realise how illusionary has been my own sense of control and identity in life; how vulnerable it is. One dreams of archetypal anima and shadow figures involved in life and death struggles and wonders to what extent their conflict is reflected within one's own life, and then as the anima projections become clearer it comes as quite a shock to realise one's own games. Clearly - to me at any rate - this dream represented the overcoming of a situation which was not right at all. The liberation of the anima points to its return to where it should be in the first place, as an underlying unconscious principle rather than as active feminising one. In subsequent dreams she has appeared as a hideous monster which has been successfully slain, as an all-wise Diotima, as a worldly courtesan, and also in these dreams the brothers, the positive and negative aspects of the male component of my psyche, have been united in their adventures.

Finally, a recent exercise in the technique of active imagination produced this fantasy:-

"I am inside a tower and sitting in the gloom of a room which looks out onto the landscape beyond. Light floods through a window so that nothing but the window itself is visible inside the room. Drawn by the light I stand up and look out, observing a gentle lakeland scene of rounded hills, meadows and a winding clear blue stream. Scrambling onto a ledge I climb out of the tower and jump to the ground below and land without coming to any harm. Walking on beyond the tower I come across the old man who greets me by raising his staff. I begin to gather up flowers from the meadow and walking on further I also meet the fair maiden from my earlier fantasy. She falls to my feet, a bit over-dramatically I think, and touching her first on her head, I lift her up. I walk on gathering flowers."

Instead of being led down into oneself in search of one's inner light or darkness, here the movement has been reversed from inner to outer and the cycle has been brought to a close with a reassertion of the outward going principle of relatedness to the outside world.

The Magic Mountain

I am not to be deceived
        by the albino maiden
The anima princess
        who gave me her ring
Four diamonds and a pearl
        signify the Self
A cave to enter in
        mindful
Of the knowledge of forms as yet unformed
Of nameless upwelling impulses

Not to be deceived by the dry sky
        over mountains
Nor by the wise old man whose guiding staff I hold
Nor by the stillness, its empty peace

Romantic poets and artists sought out such scenery
Regarding the mountains as
        dwelling places of the spirit
Fixing ascendancy to their peaks
Yearning, to their uprising thrust

But the mountain has its terrifying aspect
Communing with the maternal belly of earth
And rending down to twisted folds
        of ravines and rockfalls
No places for secure footholds

Where there is danger in unseemly movements
And where knowledge must guide the traveler

The symbols belie literalness
Upturn the matter of fact or commonplace
        Ascendancy presages fall
Descent into oneself brings discovery
        and transcendence
A journey into death
        brings rebirth

Our hubris mocks shadowy places
Naming as myth the Elysian fields and River Styx
        the boatman and his accompanying hands
But would such ignorance have the face to laugh
        in these matters?
Would it prove to be any preparation?

The corn tremors in the wind
Colours pulsate the fullness of flowers
        in the meadow
Light focuses the silhouettes of trees
Red bathes the river with the last
        of many dying suns[2]

With this passage of writing, which has been edited from a lengthier effort, I have attempted to convey some of the flavour of the experiences which accompanied my own voyage into inner space. Since then, however, my perspective has been changing. My visions still occur, indeed they are becoming if anything sharper and more

---

[2] This poem was revised in 1985. See Appendix.

vivid, but they seem less important to me. Compiling this paper must produce a distorting effect, because it has been so selective an endeavour and if one were to set out to create a more realistic narrative, more should be included. Nevertheless, it represents my own personal and solitary collision with the work and ideas of Jung. It has been, to say the least, a very stormy collision. Approaching and understanding Jung's work requires a good deal of effort and there are many occasions at which one wonders whether or not one is being led astray and that even the most beautiful and promising images gained from, say, the I Ching, might prove to be part of an elaborate cosmic hoax. However, I regard such experiences not as an end in themselves but as preparatory for a change in attitudes. Once one makes the conceptual adjustments dictated by the experience of such phenomena as synchronistic events, one wonders what the fuss was all about, but at the same time one knows only too well what it was about; unlearning one's acquired conceptual garbage. This side of the divide it all looks rather easy, but of course it isn't.

Working through the Jungian literature, together with encountering the other strands of late modernism and post-modernism, provides us with a preparatory grounding for a re-embracing of the spiritual dimension. From a point of rejecting rationalism as too unrealistic an attitude in the face of the contradictory nature of our experience of ourselves, to the point of this re-embracing, some kind of discipline is required in order to avoid becoming disorientated. I don't think it is a matter of belief, but rather one of experience, and if our intellectual framework is too narrow, we cannot get to the other end. We remain insensitive to ourselves and insensitive to the quantum foam of phenomena we participate in. We find that we have to lose preconceptions and be suspicious of definitions and chartings of this territory, because "spiritual" in this sense is not the same as in the terms we thought of before our act of re-embracing. It simply connotes a wider view of reality and not a narrower one. It does not make us less rational, but on the contrary, more so, as we embrace the crazy logic of the oriental traditions.

Intellectually I remain very uneasy about Jung's work, but then with an output which is so vast one can be both satisfied and dissatisfied with it at the same time. Yet the territory he maps out provides a key or entry point into areas one would previously have regarded as exotic, difficult or too obscure to bother with, and with that, life is not simply enriched and enhanced, but it makes more sense. The caveats that he enters into so frequently, especially in *The Relations Between the Ego and the Unconscious*, are caveats which apply when the territory is approached from too narrow a point of view; when petty rationalism collides with magic and cannot survive the encounter. Because the two appear to be irreconcilable we might tend to suspend disbelief and approach the visionary realm with the attitude of witnessing a miracle. We have had a little vision and we think we have jumped into the cosmic ocean. But the ocean is there, reaching back through our history and it is there in the history of other cultures. Yet if we do not jump overboard I think something more exciting is in the making. If we avoid being seduced by the fantasy world of the unconscious and avoid the portentousness of the Nietzschean psychosis, we have the prospect of attaining to some degree of sanity, and not to what we previously mistook for it, namely the anaesthetisation of consciousness through self-imposed and culturally conditioned restrictions.

Voyage into Night

I came into this world as if in a dream
Hallucinating to the stars at night
Dark visions of our lady
Holding the torch
It was distant and frightening
To sense one's progression so
Voyaging into night

In the dark there is no fear
It is peopled by the merry-go-round kaleidoscope
Round and round go the vistas
Unfolding
A strange entertainment
Stealthily between the sheets

One night came a twist
I was unreachable
Voyaging alone
Sentient creature caught between good and evil
Their faces
Mocking my loneliness in the night

The jerk into it
Comes suddenly
Think pleasant thoughts
Abate this restlessness

Dying is in the wrong tense
With it comes an unfolding
Too easy and too gentle
When there is no unfolding
Only it is the whiplash

I cannot recall it
Distanced as I am
Caught up in the act of living
The only unfolding

The Quest for Gold

1

Ariel

"Ariel who?"

The name seemed unfamiliar when mispronounced by my secretary. Ariel G-------. I had met him a few days back outside Edgware Road Station and had asked him to ring me at the office so that I could arrange to take him to an exhibition of my company's work at the National Gallery. He had been in a rarely communicative mood, giving me an entrée into his life which he had previously withheld. Hitherto, our acquaintance had been confined to the casual, ultra-casual, level of bar talk. A companionship of some ten years standing, but one which was totally lacking in substance. After all that time, I am surprised that I still know so little about him, but during this chance encounter he had been really excited and wanted to convey that to me. He had previously told me that he was writing a novel which brought together what he had learnt from the work of Jung and a study of the I Ching. I knew that much, but had dismissed the communication out of hand. People constantly tell me that they are doing this, that and the other, and being that sort of person myself, I view their claims with some scepticism. I was intrigued by Ariel's putative novel, however, especially since it coincided with my own interests, but I doubted whether he possessed the sustaining effort and discipline required to make it work; whether he could withstand the isolation of being an artist, of standing apart.

Ariel told me that he is a solicitor, but even that is something that I did not automatically accept.

In that vein, I almost took the view that anything he says is bound to be hyperbole. On the station platform he told me, for instance, that he is about to appear in a film and was going to trek over to California. "With a name like that," I thought, "he ought to be an actor." It sounds plausible. I can almost accept that.

"Ariel G------- on line three."

I took the call, being sufficiently intrigued to take him seriously for once. Sufficiently intrigued, because he was stepping out of the habitual pattern of our non-relationship. Something also told me that my own interests could in some way be served by our conversation; a hunch that it might lead somewhere, or to a break in my own self-defences. Having been awake all weekend, working on a presentation deadline, I was in need of some comic relief.

"When can I see you? What is your schedule? Can we meet?" I wasn't quite sure.

"Well, I will tell you what I am doing today, and we can perhaps fit each other in somewhere. First of all, I'm going to see my sex therapist, because I have a slight problem with my penis. You see, it's shrinking. I don't know what to do about it, because it's only two inches long and it's something of an embarrassment to me. He's an Indian, and very good. I rather think that he is going to play a flute, like a snake charmer, and that my prick is going to grow with the music. Do you think it will work? Tee hee! - But that's not what I've rung you about.

No, after that I'm going to the Tate Gallery with Nicholas. He's writing a piece on that lunatic Swiss Artist. And then I'm going to see David H-------, and then all hell will let loose. Darling, from tomorrow, it will be in all the papers; the biggest public relations exercise ever. And from then on, I'll just disappear. I'm going to America to talk money, and then to Saudi where they're setting me up in the Linkman Corporation. From then onwards it's just plonk, plonk! They're going to put me down like a chess piece, and every city I land in is going to have its own branch of Linkman.

So when can we meet?"

It was the enunciation which gave him credibility, the John Gielgud voice, although looking back, it was a preposterous outburst into my day. It was so preposterous that it could almost have been true. But it was Ariel's excitement which proved to be the most captivating part of his conversation. A sort of psychotic agitation which spoke of breakthroughs and things falling into place. Lunatics are people I do not dismiss, least of all those who lay claim to have access to high finance. My Achilles heel, money, had been engaged. For after all, most of the millionaires I have met have something unbalanced and monomaniacal about them. They can have the same creative lunacy as artists, and the same egomania. Money doesn't have a very precise meaning to me either. Percentages, all those zeros, millions of pounds; I'm servicing them with packages of work, and being engaged in it, it is totally unreal to me - no more than an abstraction. Money has no reality of its own; it is as unreal as the babble of a psychotic.

"When can I see you? Tell me what you are doing today, and then maybe we can meet and talk about your painting. I can get some finance together for you to get on with it, you know. But right now, I must get out. The phone doesn't stop ringing. *So,* when can we meet?"

"Well, I know how you feel Ariel. The phone hasn't stopped ringing here either. At the moment we're constantly being badgered by the press over the exhibition, but if you have the chance, do go down to the N------- Gallery. I'd like to hear what you think. I don't think that in any case you need me to take you. And then, when you've finished all your bits and pieces, I suggest that we get together some time tonight. I've got a hospital appointment in Paddington and can drop round afterwards."

Ariel suggested that he would be delighted to come and hold my hand during my blood tests, but having declined the offer, I arranged our rendezvous for later.

Another reason for my being sympathetic to Ariel at this juncture lay, as I said, in the fact that I hadn't slept for two days. It made me susceptible. Missing sleep has been one of the occupational hazards of my lifestyle for many years now, and whilst it has its creative benefits and allows me to get through the work of a week in a couple of days, it does have the disadvantage that there comes that dreadful moment of jaggedness when you are close to the edge, close to losing your cool. You begin to feel paranoid or start dreaming whilst you are still awake. But it's a feeling that can be dispelled very quickly. Experience has taught me that it is difficult to feel paranoid on a full stomach, and a slap-up meal after an all-nighter, or succession of all-nighters, brings on the natural fatigue which has been held until then in abeyance. Ariel had rung me just prior to that slap-up meal and his enthusiasm coincided with my feeling ragged, making me want to be carried away on the wave of his fantasies. Even so, what it also coincided with was my feeling that just about anything is possible. Just as I take a suspicious view of what people tell me about themselves, equally I take the view that fantastic as it may be, it can also be true. Was it really happening for Ariel? Was the bastard going to get there before I do? Was he going to take me along with him?

The novel. The film. The corporation. You can link them together in a chain of association.

Rearrange the pieces, playing a psychological chess game, and like mental association, power is a very peculiar phenomenon. It likes to attract things to it, so that things happen together and so that people become drawn into its lines of force. For that reason, it is not impossible to achieve a kind of grand-slam overnight success, although that tends to overlook the preparatory work behind such an emergence; the gathering together of trends and influences. So Ariel's outburst excited me because it indicated that something was going to happen to him. Linkman was just a symbol of that, but it could also have been a real-life business corporation as well.

I never succeeded in making my rendezvous with him that evening, and since his phone was constantly engaged I was unable to forewarn him that I might be delayed. In the event, an industrial dispute prolonged my check-up, forcing me to wait for several hours, and so I was not unduly surprised or disappointed to find Ariel out when I arrived at his apartment block three hours later than anticipated.

The building itself had been difficult to find, being located down an oppressive and dark Marylebone side street. It gave the appearance of awaiting demolition and also of being the sort of building that one would almost expect to find derelicts, drug addicts and prostitutes living in. This initial impression was contradicted, however, by the smart entry phone and the expensive designer blinds behind the windows of a second floor apartment. There was even a Mercedes limousine parked outside the main entrance.

By the time I made it into the office, the following day, I had almost succeeded in forgetting about Ariel. It was now Tuesday, the second day of a typically congested week of reports, meetings, negotiations and phone calls. Within this atmosphere, there is scant time for fantasies of the kind that Ariel was engaging in, unless of course they actually have an outcome in reality, for my projects and deadlines are already insane enough. With this in mind, I was somewhat taken aback then to find that he had already rung me three times before my arrival and was on the line to me no sooner than I had sat down with the first coffee of the working day.

"Why didn't you come?"

I explained as best as I could.

"Please see me tonight. Do come, because if I don't see you tonight I might not see you again. I am going over to America tomorrow and after that I won't be in the country again for a long time. By the way, have you seen the papers? It was clever, wasn't it? Not a word about Linkman. We suppressed the news in order to create an even bigger splash later."

By now I was getting irritable.

"I promise I will see you tonight, but I can't give a precise time. It might be late, so I'll ring when I'm free. I suggest we then go on to my club afterwards for some entertainment."

But Ariel wasn't going to let me off the hook that easily.

"Why do you think I talked to you about Linkman? I knew you would be titillated as soon as I mentioned money. Because I know something that you don't know, about you, your company and what you're doing. Why don't you send me your company Prospectus? Believe me, I can fix it. I can make anything happen for you. So come tonight!"

Once again, the arrangement to meet fell victim to the way my days tend to grow like topsy. I became waylaid by my Senior Partner into a drinking session which expanded into several bottles of champagne. On leaving, I mentioned Ariel's news about Linkman.

"I think that he's having a nervous breakdown, but I'm going to check it out and see how he is. You never know, it might even be for real. We might even find some more venture capital out of it."

At the bar, I managed another telephone conversation with him.

"I am not going to move from this apartment until you come. Do you hear? I won't move."

As the automatic door closed behind me, I found myself in a dark, tiled Victorian hallway. It was lit by a solitary electric bulb and the air was damp. There was the unmistakable odour of neglect about the place. It was the acrid smell of an unoccupied house.

Not having been greeted, I began to climb the stone stairway directly in front of me, but as I was on my way up to the first floor a light came on from below illuminating the landing to the basement area. Turning around I saw Ariel standing at the bottom of the stairs with an apologetic expression on his face, with his arms held above his head in a gesture of mock surrender.

"My God, what have you done to yourself?"

In the unflattering light of the hall Ariel looked like a helpless little middle-aged man who was having a nervous breakdown.

"What have you done to your face?"

"I've been playing cowboys and Indians. Do you want to

come and play?"

Ariel had painted his face and all the visible parts of his body red, and his normally black hair had been plastered an iridescent blue. His leather jacket and jeans were in an indescribable state, covered with blotches of colour from whatever he had been painting with, and it wasn't artist's materials. Food perhaps.

As I entered the wreckage of his flat I decided to sober up fast. Even a prolonged trip on acid would not have been responsible for this bizarre shambles of upturned tables and chairs and broken domestic items. Artistically the effect could have been more interesting, in spite of the fact that the walls had been painted with murals: incoherent splodges of yellow, red and green had been splattered across the room and were clearly the result of some kind of frenzy of action painting.

"I'm sorry about the mess and I'm afraid I've drunk the last of the champagne. As you can see I've just had a bath in it. Why didn't you bring someone else with you? It would have been fun to have an orgy."

Having taken another look at the place, I decided that it could well drive me mad as well. The two rooms, kitchen and toilet were so small that the place positively reeked of claustrophobia. It also reeked of urine; a strong, sickly smell which I found it difficult to get used to. Nevertheless, I couldn't very well leave. There had been too much of a build-up for that and so I decided to stay as long as was practical and to see what, if anything, I could do for Ariel. It certainly wasn't very promising, and attempting to clear the mess for him would have been a futile task, given the fact that he was hell-bent on wrecking everything around him for as long as this "trip" would last. Books and papers, gramophone records, magazines and photographs covered virtually the entire surface of the living room floor, and not having anywhere to sit I moved on to the kitchen where the mess was at least a trifle more acceptable. It simply looked as though nothing had been cleaned or moved for several months.

Sitting on a stool, with his back to the kitchen window, Ariel's appearance, with his painted face and tangled blue hair, was impressive. He looked like a primitive; like one of those natives of New Guinea you come across in the pages of an issue of National Geographic magazine. His ritual smearing of himself and his upturned flat weren't simply destructive or random gestures, but ordered in a crazy, infantile way. It was as if he was reaching back through the centuries and through the veneer of respectability and culture he normally projects to the state of mind of the primitive; back to wonderment and a capricious sense of humour. I didn't, as a result, feel sorry for him in this state. In his company I felt like an anthropologist encountering one of a new tribe, making notes, observing and memorising the streaks of reddish brown paint which had collected in the folds and wrinkles of his face and which made him look remarkably healthy; as if he was smeared with a facial ointment.

"Do you want to see what my sex therapist has done for me? I thought he was going to play a magic flute and make my prick rise like a cobra or a piece of rope. It's still there, but it hasn't worked I'm afraid. It's still only two inches long."

He pulled open his leather jacket and unbuttoned his trousers, bringing them down to his ankles like a small child about to go to the toilet.

"Do you want to listen to my mother? Can we listen to mother? I have a tape of her. You wait, it's here."

Ariel had been on his way to see her when we had had our chance encounter at the station over the weekend. I

43

did not want to talk to him about this or find out what the connection was between that, if there was a connection, and his present state of mind, lest it provoke some fresh outburst. It was better to wait and see, and so I asked to hear the tape.

In the corner of the living room, close by the kitchen door, Ariel had assembled a collection of objects which he described as his "shrine". Pots and pans, vases filled with dead flowers and personal objects cluttered this area, which, judging by the number of cigarette butts ground into the carpet and in the many ashtrays and saucers, had served as his principal seating area since the weekend. From this corner he played his tapes on an ancient cassette recorder, chain-smoked and stared at the wall opposite him.

As he searched for the tape, I had a chance to reflect and form my first impression of the situation I now found myself in and derive what I could about him from his books and personal possessions. These were somewhat thin on the ground. Evidently, care and thought had gone into the arrangement of things before he had begun to smash them up, but he obviously lived very simply. There was little sign of accumulation, or of the deliberate projection of his personality into his environment. The books, however, were familiar territory to me; the work of C.G. Jung, Cavafy's poems, which Ariel had introduced me to eight years back, and Doris Lessing novels, all jumbled up amongst personal papers and pornographic magazines. Looking at this selection was a depressing experience, because they were not the books of an educated man, but the props of someone who uses books in a careless and casual way. Rather oddly perhaps, I felt more concerned at the state of the books than I did about Ariel. I had a feeling that he had entered into heavy territory without understanding what he had embarked upon. It struck me that he had been playing a game of psychological Russian roulette with himself and that his present condition was a reflection of that; that he just couldn't cope with the new mental territories opened up by his fantasies and dreams and that he had become obsessed by them. Holed up in his diminutive flat, with no outlook but a dismal basement courtyard, he had become sucked into the realm of his dreams as a more attractive and alternative reality, unable to find a connection between it and his conscious personality.

Since he had failed to find the tape of his mother we listened to some music, and this helped to ease things and remove the atmosphere of tension that was developing between us. He had actually been talking continuously, although I had been listening very half-heartedly. Nevertheless, my attention picked up when he began to talk about his spiritualist. He showed me some press cuttings of her, taken from the pages of a hotel newsletter. The photographs showed her to be a thoroughly ordinary looking woman, but with the saving grace of a directness in the eyes. He also showed me a couple of her paintings, which were very amateurish indeed. They might be considered naive, but the fact of the matter was that they weren't even good. The couple I saw were rural views, showing fields and lanes with little houses, fences and gates. Even so, they were pleasing in spite of their crudity. It was as I put them down, however, that I noticed some more concealed beneath a pile of newspapers. These were in a dramatically different style and were very good indeed. I recognised them as Ariel's own.

Years ago, he told me that he occasionally painted. At that time, just about everything about him had repelled me, and the reason for that was a very simple one. Ariel was in many respects an older version of myself. A self-portrait of him in green, with lurid red eyes, hung on one of the walls of the living room. It was remarkably similar to one I had done as a student. I loathed it, but had kept hold of it, because of its self-accusatory glare which gave it a savage and expressive quality. Like Ariel, I too had written poetry, kept journals, collected my dreams and had attempted and abandoned literary projects and novels. I had been afraid of becoming like Ariel, but had learnt how to harness my paranoia for creative ends.

"What do you paint Andrew? Tell me about your painting."

"Oh mountains and hills. I paint landscapes generally, but seldom show any trees."

I broke off, because I had caught a glimpse of another of Ariel's paintings.

I should say that the paintings which first impressed me were very sludgy. Colours had been poured from the bottle and had been allowed to run into each other, creating a random, marbled effect. Then gold paint had been applied over this layer of colour to highlight it. The feeling which resulted from this was one of a luxuriant sensuality; an impression which was enhanced by the fact that the paintings had been executed on a very small scale.

But what now caught my eye was familiar to me from my own interest in the work of Jung. It was a watercolour of a tree, very symmetrically arranged, laden with fruit and dappled with gold.

"You should know what this means, Ariel, if you've read this."

I pointed to an ancient copy of one of Jung's series of lectures of the '30s.

"No, do you know about it? Please tell me."

I kept my remarks to a bare minimum. The symbol of the tree of life is not something I know a great deal about, but there was no doubt in my mind that this was what Ariel had spontaneously produced. It also encouraged me a great deal. This was the good, progressive, integrative aspect of his psyche trying to break through and I told him that much as he attempted to dip his eyelashes into a pot of gold paint, blinking and sprinkling himself with the stuff.

"That's good. Tell me some more."

"I can't tell you any more, because it's a symbol I don't have much personal experience of. All I can say is that it's a good sign."

Ariel accepted the information with a smile and took a cigarette from me before continuing with his questions.

"Do you use the I Ching?"

"Of course I do."

"But you do know more." He added, changing the subject, "Go on. Tell me."

"It's a transforming symbol. It means something is happening to you. It's about becoming whole."

There was also a very chaotically painted tree on another sheet of paper, with crazy zig-zag branches and sloppy gashes of green for the leaves. "That's a bit closer to my tree symbol," I thought. It belonged to the negative side of the psyche. Somehow I picture myself in the tree, sitting in the branches, about to be strangled by the foliage. But dark as my own tree symbol is, in real life I love trees. Yet such symbols don't have a very close relationship with our conscious lives, they belong more to the unconscious, but when they emerge spontaneously they also tell us about what lies on the threshold of consciousness. They point forward to new developments and insights, provided we can grasp their meaning.

Ariel was by now getting restless and fidgety, pestering me for cigarettes every time he had put one out. The music had gone off and the tape was virtually ripped out of the machine, hurled across the room and another one put in its place.

"Do you like my dagger?"

He produced a long blunt knife, experimented with it as something he could perhaps wear and then pointed it at me.

"No, I think we had better put that away."

I took it from him just as his voice started to come out from the cassette recorder.

"You must listen to this. That's me."

It was clear from the way the narrative was delivered that Ariel was reading from a script. You could hear him inhaling, pausing, gasping at this cigarette, with the occasional cough and turning of a page. Slow and ponderous with great emphasis on the words, the tape contained a series of memories from his childhood.

"I remember my aunt used to live in a big block of flats in Highgate called Highpoint. We used to go by bus, and my aunt would give us tea, and we would go to the roof where ... where we would have a competitions between us as to who could pee the farthest."

The thought of little boys climbing to the roof of Highpoint to pee all over this celebrated work of early modern architecture amused me no end. In fact the tape was very funny throughout, and the way in which he kept pausing in the middle of sentences made it seem more so. He would appear to be leading up to something, stop, and then veer off on another tack. It was also read in a matter of fact and official manner, as if part of one of Ariel's presentations in court.

"At the age of twelve I fell madly in love with my aunt's

husband. He was not a homosexual, but I lusted after him with a passion and vehemence I have never experienced since."

Once again the tape was taken out, but this time it was not hurled across the room, but handed to me together with several volumes of diaries.

"Can you put those over there and sort them out into some order for me? Did you really like my paintings?"

"Yes, very much. They remind me of the work of a girlfriend of mine."

As Ariel put on another tape of music I began to look through his diaries. Ordinarily I would not have thought of intruding into his privacy in this manner, but I felt very strongly that that was what I was with him for. I felt free to take from his experiences and witness them, since he was giving them to me so openly. Having said that though, I found the entries dismal. There were about five or so volumes stretching back a couple of years and the subject matter (on a random glance) appeared to be pretty consistent. Vivid sexual fantasies alternated with descriptions of dreams, as well as with very brief entries about his friends. What struck me was the sheer obsessiveness of his immersion within the world of his unconscious. These were, indeed, books of dreams.

Reading on, I was reminded of the experience friends of mine have had with drugs. Two suffered complete mental breakdowns after taking acid and a third committed suicide after prolonged abuse with any drug he could lay his hands on. I was reminded especially of the experience of one of them, Davidh. During a spectacularly bad trip he felt that a serpent was coiled up inside him, wrapping itself around the base of his spine several times. As the trip took off, the serpent released itself, shot up his spine, entered his brain and burst through his skull. It was the prelude, he said, to a six-month breakdown and several years of recovery after that. In Kundalini yoga, the serpent is taken to represent the spinal column, to which are connected the Chakras, or seats of consciousness. The process of meditation, and the increasing conscious awareness which leads from it, is said to lead to the liberation of these Chakras and the stage-by-stage progression through them. Enlightenment occurs when all the seats of consciousness have been activated, from the lowest animal instincts to the highest spiritual and transcendental level. This process is symbolised through the uncoiling and liberation of the serpent, which is generally a symbol which denotes the power of libido. From this, if one accepts that a parallel exists, Davidh had experienced a drug-induced instant enlightenment which nearly finished him off. What interested me most was that he took a very literal interpretation of what had happened to him; that there had indeed been this parasitical creature inside him, worming its way through his body. He could not, as a result of this, and as a result of the fact that it occurred through a hallucinogenic sensation, experience the serpent as a symbol. He could not bring his consciousness to it and could only recoil from it in terror. Such an enlightenment was of no value to him at the time, because he could not experience it. It, on the contrary, experienced him.

I felt that Ariel had in a way fallen victim to one of the fashions which have sprung up in the wake of psychoanalysis; the idea that if you write down your dreams and fantasies, that this will in itself prove beneficial. It may, but the critical factor remains the extent to which the symbols are understood. Another problem is created by the fact that each experience of an unconscious symbol produces its own field within which one can become trapped, unable to see its relation to the whole and mistaking it for the whole. Davidh and Ariel had thus become fascinated with the unconscious at the expense of their own conscious identities. In Ariel's case, he was pushing himself on and on, not holding back for analysis and a greater degree of self-understanding. What he had found himself in was a beautiful and bizarre and terrible and unmanageable world. He was going through something which had become necessary and would continue to be so until a change of attitude on his part occurred. He had tried to cultivate the unconscious as a pet, and it was now turning a little wild.

There remained the tape of Ariel's mother which I now prepared myself to listen to in the anticipation of being bored, but just as most of his "surprises" had proved to be entertaining ones, the tape demanded attention. It took the form of an interview between mother and son and concerned itself with the years of the War, during which he had been an evacuee.

"Mother, can you tell me about father? You once said that you thought he was carrying on with another woman."

By contrast with Ariel's Oxbridge tone, she spoke with a staunch London accent.

"Oh well, we didn't think about it in those days. Certainly you never talked about it even if it did go on - not like today - but if he was, we didn't make an issue of it. We knew what we had and we didn't complain, you see. But I loved your father. Oh yes, I did. I was very unhappy then, but it settled down and we got through it all right. A lady's man, he was a lady's man, and always so smart. He always went out with a neat suit, clean shirt ... Oh yes."

Ariel could not listen to the tape for long. He began to fidget once more, especially since we had by now got to the end of my packet of cigarettes.

"If you go to the Metropole and get some more fags I promise I'll clear this place out. When I go to America I will have a whole team of interior designers and decorators in to transform the place. You won't recognise it. Designer blinds, designer carpets! Yes, I'll be the first Buddhist millionaire! They can then make a bonfire of this lot. Now be a good boy and get me some cigarettes and then we can go to a party I've been invited to in Waterloo. They're sure to have a good orgy on there."

Leaving the flat, I became aware once more of the stench of urine and could not help wondering whether or not I would return from my errand. The temptation to leave him there was strong, but the Metropole Hotel made me overcome my momentary resistance to him. Its ersatz marble halls and nowhere-in-particular decor made me uncomfortable and anxious to leave. Businessmen in pin-striped suits and shirts were, at well past midnight, still talking business. It was that sort of place, frequented by people who have just got off planes. Altogether the walk took me twenty minutes and reminded me of how tired I now was and how anxious I was to leave.

On returning I found him in an old -fashioned Oriental dressing gown engaged in the process of cleaning the flat up. This resolution proved short-lived. Ariel's irritation with the gramophone records proved to be its undoing, for they had become splattered with paint and would no longer work. It led to another session of breaking things. Records were smashed against the player and plates were thrown against the wall and the kitchen floor. Undaunted, he then began to hurl the contents of several bags of rice about the living room.

"Shall we plant some trees? Here are the seeds. Whoeey!"

Escaping into the bedroom, I managed to find a corner

in which I could avoid the missiles. Unlike the rest of the flat, the bedroom was in a pre-breakdown state. It was actually quite well decorated, with white walls and blinds, a long, low bed and a pine wardrobe reaching across one wall. This had open shelves and compartments which revealed newly pressed suits and shirts. A fine silk shirt pointed to another side of Ariel, although it had the look of being seldom worn.

Now that the commotion had died down I decided to attempt to capitalise upon the momentary calm and get him to do something to leave.

"Let's just concentrate on getting you ready. Can you have a bath at your friends' place?"

"Oh yes, let's go. But let me do some more painting first."

Ariel returned to the kitchen and emerged with two large bottles of Hellman's mayonnaise which he brandished like guns as he began to empty their contents against the walls.

Looking for one last diversion, now that my interest in his performance was becoming exhausted, once again I came across his collection of magazines and pin-ups. Most of them were American, chunky, beefy individuals who I found strangely tame, antiseptic and un-erotic. He also had some photographs of friends he had been on holiday with to the Greek islands; the sort that you get developed privately. Like everything else in the living room, these were in a state of disarray and were mixed up with other photographs from his childhood. Some of these were no larger than stamps and had been taken directly off the negatives. This overall jumble of possessions, the tapes, records, photographs and diaries, revealed something of the background to Ariel's present state of mind. It amounted to a kind of review of his life, a sign of his own attempt at self-analysis. By now, in spite of the fact that the cumulative effect of all these items had impressed me deeply, I was anxious to leave, and unable to persuade him to clean himself up, the two of us walked on to the Edgware Road in order to find a taxi. He had by now changed back into his leather jacket and jeans, and from a distance looked relatively normal. Close to, however, he looked even more bizarre under the garish street light and his appearance deterred a number of cab drivers from taking us. When one did stop, he managed to produce his best Oxbridge manner on the principle that no matter how rough you may look, the class barriers still operate.

"Pardon me, but could you take us to The Cut in Waterloo. I must apologise for my appearance, but I've been painting. Thank you."

I, in the meantime, wanted to be put off in town, and disembarking at Leicester Square, I left him with enough money and cigarettes for the night and slipped in to my club to catch a last drink before going home. I allowed myself the luxury of not thinking as I sat watching the indifferent jazz cabaret, picking grains of rice out of my hair.

Although I had maintained a sense of detachment from Ariel's predicament, I was not altogether a stranger to it. I have experienced a great deal of mental illness in the people close to me, and whilst I have never had a breakdown myself, there have been times when I too have been close to the edge. Indeed, I have spent most of my life on that edge and have also deliberately cultivated it. Whenever I veer away from it, I actually begin to feel guilty that I am not pushing myself hard enough, and that realisation always pulls me up sharp and permits me my own brand of madness. As soon as that becomes difficult to maintain, I am pulled up once more and re-emerge from my creative wanderings into the sort of lifestyle most people accept as normal. This process works automatically as a kind of safety valve which prevents me from falling into a psychological abyss, even if feel I have stumbled into one. Ariel lacked that kind of self-righting balance, I thought, and this made him too weak to withstand the onslaught of the dreams and fantasies he had opened himself up to.

To Ariel, the life of the psyche had begun to appear more real and important than anything else. It carried too much charge with it for him to be able to pull himself immediately out of its pall. Nor could he find a socially acceptable way of going off his head by pursuing religion or mysticism as a means of structuring his experiences. He had simply fallen in. As a result of this I left him feeling disappointed, because the excitement that he initially communicated to me is also the excitement of being on the edge, of being alive and receptive to all possibilities. I was hopeful, however, that he would recover rapidly, providing that such recovery would offer to him more than his present condition. You have to have something to recover to in the same basic way as at the end of the day you need to have a home to go to, no matter how simple or inadequate. The excitement that he was experiencing, its agitation, also had its problems. It needs an outlet or a point to it. Without that, without some creative object to work upon, it can become pretty hard to stomach or ride upon; as hard as the compromise of living contained within the four blank walls of a small room.

Meeting him also reminded me of how far I had strayed away from the world of my own psyche and of how much I had closed off my own spiritual urges. That too, is an extreme position, even if it is a much more common one. It's an extreme that is only generally avoided by living in thrall to the habitual, in allowing routine to take over and live for one, because it is easier that way. Leaving him, I decided that it was time for me to re-open myself to my own experimentation and let it happen to me rather than treat it as some kind of opus, but how I would do that remained a very questionable matter, but then, the whole subject is, by its very nature, questionable.

If Ariel had been able to sustain the trip he would have made the breakthrough. He might indeed still make it, for its effects cannot be measured simply in time. The filtering through of the unconscious symbols to their conscious realisation takes many months and may even require many years to reach an outcome. It can lift individuals up and motivate them to exceptional achievements or to the stumbling upon of powerful ideas, but because of the power which is associated with the symbols, the effects of the experiment which goes wrong can also be measured. It can have a negative effect, for you may try to hold on to the energy of the psyche and make the mistake of believing that it is your own creation. It is out of that misappropriation of the psyche that the Nietzschean heresy emerges; the idea that having access to psychic powers and energy makes you more than human. Believing that simply makes you inhuman or mad.

The following day I asked my secretary to take no more calls from Ariel. I felt unable to help him in any way.

2

The Serpent

The encounter with Ariel continued to disturb and stimulate me for many weeks. It was not that the bizarre results of his experiment with himself had deeply affected me, but that it had served to remind me of all my previous explorations of the inner landscapes of my own psyche. Finding the triggering point for a re-examination of these was proving extremely difficult for me, and structuring them into some assimilable form even more so. To hold the totality of their images within the fragmentary and isolating focus of one's consciousness is an irredeemable task. For, having attempted to describe and explain them for other people and close friends who have embarked upon the experiment, I fall headlong into the traps formed by my own intellect and my tendency to intellectualise. This was driven home to me forcefully by my attempts to continue my narrative by recounting the history of one of my strongest friendships, but this relationship has proved to be so difficult to convey a flavour of that I have had to abandon that task.

John and I began working together on the manuscript of our three-year-long series of dialogues and mutual promptings, and during our analytical sessions it became obvious that the images we wished to explore could not yield their meaning through an intellectual approach, nor through a conventional descriptive narrative. He put on the tape recorder to document and play back my reading of the story of our times together and after three hours of tangential discourse and the hard and difficult work of listening to each other, we sat back and went over our conversation once more. We became passive parties to our own active and over-conscious interaction. It was the salutary shock that I had been waiting for.

During my reading I had become increasingly uncomfortable and unhappy about what I was trying to do. Writing about someone close to you and with whom you have achieved a rapport is a sensitive and potentially destructive task. That is why I had brought the manuscript to John for his approval, comments and contribution. Yet for all our shared interests in the occult and in the exploration of the psyche, I left feeling that the exercise was an irrelevant one. Together we had been working upon achieving the breakthrough to higher levels of consciousness, and for once we were becoming constipated, repeating by now over-familiar ground. Both of us acknowledged this impasse and were now concentrating upon breaking the deadlock without plunging or falling into Ariel's state of possession. We had been close enough to the edge or dividing line between sanity and madness to know that the experience of paranormal phenomena requires the most fastidious hold over consciousness. At the same time, we were intuitively working for something other than that perpetual balancing act, but as yet it is a nameless state of being which has few points of reference within our present culture. Rather than being a particular state of mind, it is a point of entry; an embarkation into another realm of time and perception. Getting there is a curious process of working through one's resistances and amplifying one's knowledge in order to build up one's confidence. Then, at the point of entry, curious things begin to happen, and the causal relationship between things is jettisoned in the free-fall. How long can you hold it? Should you go in? The gate has been opened and you peer through into other realms, cautiously testing their reality before coming to. Perhaps on the following day you are a little later than usual in getting to work, and somehow day-to-day survival becomes a little more pressing and followed more keenly. Or perhaps one day you may create an image or symbol so potent that you may disappear into it forever.

As I sat listening to our conversation, the sound of our voices jarred me into sharper concentration. John came over familiar and undistorted. A sharp, theatrical, nasal and camp voice, drawling and perpetually pausing for further thought. John aims for precision and a pedantic form. To his voice there is a mechanical edge and a sense of self-amusement which comes from savouring the projection of his own thoughts. At the same time, his delivery is highly idiosyncratic and exaggerated. I, on the contrary, had never heard myself on a recording and was appalled at the playback. Somehow my own self-perception had been violated and bore little resemblance to what I now heard. You have to live with yourself and dull your ears to your own sounds and look in the mirror carelessly and indulgently. You are so ubiquitous to yourself that you do not observe and remark upon the obvious fact that you too are an object for the thoughts and perceptions of others. I the observer was now the observed.

An intellectual, soft and educated voice confronted me. It was flat, unemphatic and lacked any excitement. It was so under-stated and cool that I could see that the whole position it maintained was a distorted and phony one. In someone else I could have tolerated and even appreciated it, but in myself, I could not, and had to admit that I bored myself. My whole approach to what I was describing had to be abandoned and the images themselves had to be left unsullied by explanations and rationales.

Another thing which disturbed me about my attempt to describe my reactions to John was that so many of our stages of development had occurred in the past. They were something that we had worked through together and something we were progressing away from. Going over them, no matter how personally relevant they were, was no longer a concern of the present and they had consequently become redundant. Concentrating upon them had appeared to be a good idea, but doing so was in fact holding me back. This became only too apparent during our conversation about the writing. It was clear that it could not be used as a means of getting to the point of entry and that in order to give an expression to the experience of that threshold you have to be there in the first place, living within the world of its images. That realisation depressed me and posed a more serious challenge. Accepting that was a recognition of the necessity of living within a dual world, between fantasy and reality, whilst maintaining a firm grip on both and a sense of the differentiation between them. It might appear to be like risking an encounter with madness in order to gain a greater degree of sanity and a greater awareness of reality.

Many things had changed for John since I had first met him. No longer was he living in squalid or disorganised surroundings, and his lifestyle was no longer quite that of an itinerant who rarely settles in one place for long. A cutting table, sewing machine and battery of lights to work under, emphatically proclaimed his trade. There was a feeling of his having settled and of his deliberate cultivation of an atmosphere geared to an easy combination of work and relaxation. To a tailor's dummy was pinned the beginnings of a complicated asymmetrical gown in white silk chiffon; an attempt at a definite aesthetic and personal statement about form. Fragments of an Art Deco mirror were carefully displayed on the fireplace wall and beside them, photographs of himself and various other possessions of a talismanic character. The room was his magical chamber and was gradually being saturated with the signs and presences of his personality. All this was in marked contrast to my past knowledge of him during times at which his personality had veered perilously close to disintegration.

We were joined for our conversation by his lover, Michael, and his nervous but thoughtful movements made me feel uneasy. In the past, the friendship with John had been an exclusively one-to-one intellectual exchange into which others had only ventured by invitation. The energy and concentration which we had applied to each other was often so intense that there was insufficient room left for another to share our company. Indeed, without a word said, we had regularly taken each other away from other companions who were frightened or put off by the directness of our intimacy. For a long time now there had been few holds barred between us and no desire or need for conflicts or changes in viewpoint. Where differences had occurred, resolutions were speedily arrived at through the realisation that we had simply understood each other badly or insufficiently. However, that intimacy did not stem from any desire to possess each other or deny ourselves other outlets, friendships and relationships. We did not want anything from each other, and hence had an instinctive and empathic awareness of each other's needs and moods. Nor did that mean that we were entirely similar either. John always was a little bizarre and non-conformist in appearance and behaviour, often verging on going over the top and being outrageous, whereas I, by comparison, could be described superficially as bourgeois, conservative and acceptable. Nevertheless, Michael's presence proved to be highly useful for me in subjecting my description of John to a third party and crucial in making me realise its irrelevance for our purposes. It was also badly written, for its intentions were unclear and too rooted in what we knew already. There was no need for descriptions and analyses of the telepathic, synchronistic and visionary phenomena we had experienced, for their truth lies in the experience itself and its engendering.

Before we had begun our session, John handed me a pack of Tarot cards. They were designed for Aleister Crowley's use. As I looked through them, I was greatly impressed by their beauty and power. They were no ordinary designs, but produced out of a deep insight into the workings of the unconscious and out of a knowledge of other traditions, religions and symbolic systems. I meditated upon them and realised that they would require a great deal of study in order to gain access to their meaning and full power. They were real and genuine symbols, for each one radiated an almost tangible energy. They are transforming symbols, which by their nature, induce change in the personality of their possessor.

Much of John's present stability and confidence I felt was due to Michael, to his attentiveness, tolerance and sheer introversion. In contrast to John's wordiness, he remained silent and ventured only the occasional remark. However, drained after all our talk it was good to turn to him and be shown his paintings and drawings. I looked at them warily, with the eye of someone who is both an artist and a businessman. That Michael found his work difficult and often painful was obvious. By many standards the paintings were naive and lacking in confidence, but the principal feature which gave them an interest to me was their mythological subject matter. Michael too was inhabiting the world of his dreams; an extraordinarily colourful, emotional and charged one of archaic gods and goddesses, orgyastic rites, buddhas and classical statues and gardens. At least three of the paintings were superbly controlled and integrated. In them a balance had been achieved between the energy and vibrance of the dream landscape and the references of composition. In the others, the energy had led to a kind of visual incoherence or broken speech.

Gradually, as we continued our conversation and smoked a couple of joints, I slid further into my depression and sense of failure. Overcome by fatigue, I felt unable to leave for a planned visit to a Halloween night party. It was all hopeless, and I felt as though I was 50 and not 28. The sound of my voice irritated me, John's voice irritated me and Michael's wheezes and sneezes from a cold also irritated me. It was by now clear from his manner that Michael wanted me to leave. A knife placed in front of you, facing towards you, amounts to no less. John said,

"What I love about Mike, is that he is so marvelously unconscious. You can say what you like to him and he will come out with these things which grab you by the scruff of your neck and hit you where you need it. He's much brighter than he lets onto."

I left feeling disorientated and punch-drunk. The marijuana had made me lose my sense of direction. I felt as though I was walking backwards whilst going forwards, and abandoning the effort, jumped into a taxi and went on to the party where I was so totally unconnected that I wandered about looking lost and dispossessed. The drug was mildly hallucinogenic, and in the smoke-filled rooms, devils' faces leered at me through their masks and simulation blood dripped convincingly as my imagination took hold of me. In a state of stupor, I was apathetic at the prospect of leaving and facing another day. It was the summation of the mood of several weeks. Six weeks of inexorable break-up since my meeting with Ariel. It was becoming painful.

News of Ariel had filtered through to me via his friends. One told me unsympathetically and coldly that he was having a breakdown, and the latest of many at that. Since the communication was neither warm nor concerned I dismissed it, but when I met Vasilis at a loud and crowded disco, the response was a positive one. An old friend of Ariel's he was more forthcoming.

"Why don't you see Ariel? Go and see him," he shouted over the booming noise.

This was impossible. We were screaming down each other's ears, exasperated by the excessive level of the music. Misunderstanding followed upon misunderstanding.

"Why are you afraid? Go and see Ariel. He needs to see people now."

I explained that I could not see him, because I would not be able to communicate.

"He was too cracked up when I saw him last."

Vasilis threw up his hands and gesticulated his disgust.

"Ariel cracked? Never! You listen to me, you just listen to me. It's your problem. It's not Ariel's."

"I know it's my problem," I replied.

"It's your problem. You don't have to worry about Ariel. No one has to worry about Ariel. He is being looked after well. Look, Ariel has achieved levels of consciousness you will never experience. He has beautiful things inside his head. Ariel is beautiful, do you hear?"

I agreed. Vasilis continued his explanation.

"To do what Ariel has done requires great strength. Very few people can do it and survive. And he has many problems, and to go through what he is going through ..."

For a few moments Vasilis was unable to continue. It struck me as symptomatic of the last decade that we had spent all this time in crowded bars, nightclubs and discotheques shouting our conversations at each other over the level of noise, snatching at fragments of each other and unable to experience anything closer. Somehow through Ariel we were becoming more involved with each other. He was acting as a pivotal point.

Vasilis handed me his card.

"Don't worry about Ariel. Give me a ring, and we will go and see him."

Then, a couple of weeks after this exchange, I met Ariel himself in another nightclub, accompanied by another old friend, who I know only as "Tulip". He was looking drained, but also radiant, and the clothes which I had last seen him in were now thoroughly cleaned up. We said little, but laughed a great deal through a video of Bette Davis and Joan Crawford torturing each other in "Whatever happened to Baby Jane?"

"You look beautiful. Are you in love?" he asked.

In the weeks that had followed my visit to Ariel's flat, I was finding it increasingly difficult to maintain the fine divide between following creative goals and coping with a demanding and difficult job. Taking advantage of a temporary lull in my business schedules had become absolutely necessity, for I was in desperate need of a rest in order to put my head in order and untie the mess that the chapter on John had got into. I had put aside but a week to achieve that. Ordinarily I could paint or write or comfort myself with domestic chores, but now it became obvious to me that I had landed myself in a thorough impasse. Little by little, I was unable to keep a hold on myself and my deadlines. I was torn between the two extremes of returning to my job and my projects and of carrying on with an introspection which was threatening to undermine my meteoric career rise. I could not decide which was the more important and which the more unreal to me. The interior landscape, or the equally bizarre world of business personalities, committees and multi-million pound deals. It seemed to me that the balancing act had now become a never-never land, a disconcerting state of limbo. It had become disembodied and disconnected from the reality of both my worlds.

John had recognised this predicament with his usual perception. He told me that in order to achieve the point of entry I would have to put myself or my protagonists through a process of disintegration, through the break-up of Ego. Now, however, I felt that this balance between a disintegration of Ego and a re-integration of my personality was going to elude me, and that nothing more glamorous than a straightforward collapse was awaiting me.

In this mood of desperation, I walked out early one Wednesday morning onto the Common which my house overlooks, to watch the mist rise from its fields and hear the rattle of the first commuter trains. Autumn was late in coming. It was still mild enough to be in shirt sleeves, and the chestnut trees were still in leaf. The magpies, crows and wood pigeons had long since stirred. A great congregation of about 20 crows had gathered in the largest field, and with each step I took through the rain drenched and muddy grass, those closest to me took flight and regrouped themselves further away from me. This ensemble successfully managed to maintain its formation despite the constant swooping and gliding of the birds as they escaped my advance towards them. Finally, they had come to the edge of the field, and with nowhere else to reform, they rose up en masse and took to the tops of the oak trees which line the railway. Somehow their flight seemed comical and clumsy, all the more so as when landing on the topmost branches they came perilously close to falling off, the trees bending and swaying under their ungainly weight. They looked marvelously unconscious and oblivious; fat, contented and complacent; I, by contrast, felt my spiritual weariness keenly as I selected a tree to sit under. I felt that I was ready to reach the point of entry and felt indifferent to all the things I was about to leave behind.

When John was seriously ill as a result of poisoning himself after a suicide attempt, I had told him that I knew how to reach that point. You have to genuinely feel uncluttered and unfettered by this world and be fully sated with it. Whatever you are leaving behind must involve no residues and left over resolutions. Even the things you have left undone must be utterly abandoned and their lack of completion tasted to the bitter full. In that way, you can let go and give to everything an equivalence, between failure and fulfilment.

As I sat cross-legged and concentrated upon the emptiness and the non-conscious clear spaces within my head, I realised that my desperation was also a phony one. It was part of a natural rhythm, the diapason of my swings of mood. Such troughs have always been followed by periods of great activity and creativity, and all that remained was to ride it out and follow it through. My will for life and zest for it continued to be insatiable, and my hunger and thirst were all too real. As I meditated I held on once or twice to the emptiness, and to its stillness, but with each sound of an animal stirring next to me, a squirrel ferreting for nuts or a hedgehog pushing its way through the undergrowth, my attention slipped. Hovering between concentration and non-concentration, I allowed my mind to form pictures before me in the grey overcast sky. The clouds became a stormy sea as I rushed towards them in my imagination. Through them a causeway spread into the distance. Waves pounded the rocks and threatened to erode my foothold, rising into great swirling arches before falling back again into the sea. By now the sky was darkening through grey to black, with great banks of cloud mounting rapidly and menacingly with the commotion of wind and rain. A gale was blowing up and my progress across the causeway was becoming increasingly dangerous, as the water had by now covered it. At this point it was no longer possible to distinguish between the sea and the land. Everything had become one as the spray from the water swelled up with the crushing and pounding of the waves. As I walked on, the heaving of water subsided and ahead of me lay land: a steaming and foggy bog within which the only distinguishable features were a solitary and withered tree, and behind it, a mound of earth, out of which smoke was rising as if from a quenched fire. I remember thinking that this place was in fact more dangerous than the sea which had led me onto it. It was more like an island. Perhaps it was Böcklin's Isle of the Dead.

Out of the mist forms became recognisable. I had already encountered them on many occasions throughout my childhood and adolescence, and they were already known to me from my deepest moments of meditation. They were revenants, cast-off spirits of the graveyards and other damp and damned places. I was not afraid, for I knew their function well as guardians of the holy territories ordinarily and necessarily inaccessible to idle adventurers.

If you cannot withstand the encounter with them you will run off like a terrified child, or you may be consumed by them, or you may accept rationalistic explanations from the sources of psychology. Freud called them personifications of the Id, the unruly or childish aspects of the unconscious mind, but when you are haunted by them, no amount of psychoanalysis will ease their terror; the terror of encountering their dangers and emerging as the victorious hero.

Just as the only way you can encounter pain is by facing it head on and refusing to dull it with tranquillisers and refusing to run away from it, these demons demand full and open acknowledgement, and a recognition of their point of origin within us as kindred spirits. They are a part of us, one and the same, and a failure to see that opens up the path towards a full possession by them. Howling female figures with gaping bloody mouths shrieked above me and disappeared into the mist, only to re-emerge again as more dreadful skeletal chimaeras. Half beast, half woman, they danced on revealing their open sores, cavorting their Grand Guignol ballet. Beyond them, nameless creatures crawled on the earth with furry backs and leathery tentacles, spreading feelers and suckers as they moved on laboriously. One of them metamorphosed itself into a huge scorpion, larger than a coffee table. Altogether there were hundreds of these creatures lurking in the swamp. At a glance they looked surprisingly and memorably real, so that if you reached out and touched one, with the swipe of a bladed limb your hand would disappear in the encounter. One settled on my shoulder and made to bite my neck as I brushed it off.

As I reached the tree I came across a dip in the ground, and in the hollow beyond a man emerged from the shadows. It was not quite human. Bellowing silently and furiously, it was bent double in pain. Moving closer to it, I could see that it was a combination of man and machine. Its head was crudely attached and its face was like a curious science fiction mask, incapable of registering the emotion and pain it was feeling in its coming to consciousness, bereft of the nuances of expression.

At the summit of the peaty tumulus I could see that the smoke was coming from a cauldron, which on a closer examination was glowing red hot. Crackling and sizzling noises both surrounded it and appeared to be coming from it. Darting movements of air and smoke around its base alerted me to a fresh presence. I found myself directly in the line of its guardian. Its thick scaly coils glistened in the moisture of the morning. Like the air and the surrounding landscape it was also grey, but in the increasingly clear light of the day it radiated brilliant multi-coloured flashes from its scales. Palpable and breathing, I wanted to reach out and touch its coils, concealed within which I knew lay its head. The serpent stirred, and as it did so its coils slid effortlessly and noiselessly against each other, parting to reveal not one, but several heads. The cauldron was guarded by a hydra. I reached out and placed my hand on its back, stroking the scales to bring them to lie flat in a gesture of placation. I was to pass.

Once before the cauldron I could see that this too was not what it appeared to be. It was not cast from metal, but consisted of some organic material. It was indeed alive. As I stood there it began to move, at first slowly, rotating gently, gyrating about its base and gradually rising upwards. Reaching the level of my eye, it began to tilt towards me, continuing to make circular movements. For the first time I felt hesitant, for as its tilting continued, I saw that I had good reason to feel less confident. The whole cauldron itself was none other than a gigantic mouth, armed with great rings of teeth.

It was the head of a huge worm, and the tumulus upon which the serpent lay coiled was its belly. As I looked into it, the teeth retreated into an opening which circled its mouth, and directly above me it began to spew out its contents. Countless gold coins rained out onto me. I had found the treasure.

I walked on along a footpath where the Common is pinched to a narrow slither of land, into a left-over space wedged between the railway, the back gardens of suburban houses and the grounds of the local boys' school. In this quiet corner you get the solitary walkers with their dogs, horses taken out for exercise and elderly ladies on their way back from shopping expeditions. As a child this was my favourite place. Somewhere to explore, along the line of fences, picking out stones, broken fragments of pottery and other discarded items which were to be horded away. Here I remembered the overgrown ditch which you have to negotiate carefully whilst wading through the grass, feeling for it with my feet before jumping over into the wooded portion by the fences. Normally no one goes here, and now that my mind was clearing I hoped that I would remain alone, but the abruptness of my movements in clearing the ditch disturbed a middle-aged man who had been peering through a gap at the children in the school playing field beyond.

Nothing of great importance happened to me for the rest of the day and the vision itself was dismissed as soon as it had disappeared. Its significance took several hours to filter through as I relaxed over a bath, many cups of coffee and letters that I discarded as soon as I had written them. If I had found the treasure, what then was the treasure? How would it materialise from this encounter with the serpent? Unable to find an answer that satisfied me, I went over in my mind the plans for the next day, which were for a trip to Canterbury Cathedral with a friend who was preparing to conduct a lecture tour there. I was in two minds as to whether I should go with him, for the intensity of our past relationship was returning at the very point at which it had appeared to be receding. I prevaricated, rang to cancel the arrangement, and then rang again to say that I wanted to go after all.

"Forgive me, but I'm very confused at the moment. I do want to go, but I wish we weren't so bloody scared of each other."

For once, Terence's telephone manner was positive and assertive and amounted to a demand for me to go there with him in spite of all our scenes together.

He was late. I looked at him closely and intensely. Broken blood vessels on the cheeks, he was looking pale and uncharacteristically ill. He was also inadequately dressed for the journey. We were at Victoria Station on a cold November morning and had just missed a train. So we sat drinking coffee, waiting for the train, looking at each other and making deadpan conversation, easing hesitantly towards a point of safety and mutual respect, if such a thing were possible between us.

Our approach to Canterbury was remarkably thorough. We bought the guidebooks and walked around the City and its Cathedral, reading passages to each other as we studied their treasures, and filling in from our own knowledge the things which are not said in such worthy volumes. At the City Walls we climbed the Dane John Mound where two spiral ramps snake their way to a late Neoclassical monument upon its summit. It was erected in 1803 to the memory of a local banker who had provided the money for the gardens which lie around its base, but upon the inscriptions which commemorate these facts there is no mention made of the age or purpose of the mound and the visitor might be excused for thinking that it is a folly. Its neatly clipped hedges, grass and graveled paths, and the precisely sculpted monument, point to the Georgians' love of "improvement", especially when in pursuit of the picturesque. The folly is in reality an ancient burial mound which has been tidied up, but the monument is very fine and reminded me of the cauldron and the worm. A castellated Gothic base supports a slender Tuscan Doric column, which is capped by a Grecian urn.

Canterbury was splendidly alive in a way which is only possible when you are looking through two pairs of eyes, constantly coming across things you would have missed if alone, and not having been there before, I was particularly struck by the way in which the atmosphere of the Cathedral had been preserved as a place of repose. The church is just rooted there, a great mass of stone which has been worked upon by countless hands and gradually eroded by the elements. It is the great opus; an intellectual, emotional and spiritual work, the deep symbolism of which seldom penetrates our modem rationalism.

I was standing by the South-West Tower and its face was covered with scaffolding. New stone was being laid, and as I waited for Terence to return from the Deanery Office where he had gone to seek permission for his tour, I felt a distaste for all that cheap looking new stone. It was mechanical and precise and executed without a love for the work. When he did return, he was complaining of the cold, hoping that he wasn't going to suffer from another pleurisy relapse. I held his hand, which was icy. As I looked up, I remembered a dream I had had in which I was a mason called in to restore the tower of another great cathedral. It was situated at the top of a hill, overlooking a valley and at the end of an avenue of trees. I knew that the cathedral represented the summit of consciousness and was a symbol for the work of consciousness, and its soaring an expression of the aspiration to rise up from the valley and the worldly things within it.

I began the work as a young man, and toiling away through its stages I was not aware of the passage of time and my own inexorable ageing and decay. The tower absorbed me, for it was a microcosm of our cultural history. Built on Roman foundations, its base and porch, with their chevron etched arches, were Norman, and from them, reticent lancet windows pointed upwards to form a second stage or level. At the third stage, a great festooned and decorated arch proclaimed the confidence of the gothic masons, with gargoyles and grotesques projecting from the springing point of its columns. By my 55th year I had reached the open late Gothic belfry, and all that remained was the relatively simple task of repairing the timbers and lead of a baroque dome which capped the tower, but it was a task that I could not stomach. Rather than touch that stylistic aberration, I succumbed to a prolonged attack of vertigo which rendered me incapable of climbing to such heights again. At least I could be pensioned off and live to enjoy the results of my work, for masons who become habituated to the dangers of their task tend to plunge to the base of their scaffolding and die slowly from broken and twisted limbs. That was indeed the fate of William of Sens, the master of the early Gothic choir at Canterbury.

The Cathedral at Canterbury also takes you through a layer cake of history. Anselm's Norman church is still visible in the crypt, the Treasury and the Easternmost

Transepts, which form the exterior remain relatively untouched by the later Gothic additions. Here the arches and masses of plain unadorned wall cling to their Roman and antique heritage. Distorted as their proportions are, the grammar is still Classical, and it is to this part of the church that I gravitate. Its simplicity is deceptive, for the arches hide lush Corinthian columns and keystone motifs from the Eastern Mediterranean. Even the apsidal bays of the Transepts are distinctly Byzantine.

In the crypt we studied the tombs and the rich carvings on the column capitals. The latter are probably the greatest treasures of Canterbury, and yet they are obscured by the partitioning to an exhibition area. The insensitivity of their concealment behind unsightly perspex screens points to the incomprehension by the modern church of their archaic and rich symbolism. These are things which the secular clerics have disregarded in their embarrassment, for they are riddled with paradoxes and signs of an arcane understanding. By one of these, I pointed out to Terence the meaning of some of the symbols which I recognised, and as I did so, he became uncomfortable. To be told, against your Christian assumptions, that the Devil and Christ are but aspects of the same force is an unsettling experience, no matter how tenuous your hold over the inculcated religion may be, but one of these columns tells the story with great mastery and with the utmost precision, so that there can be little doubt as to the dual aspect of its symbols. Masonic ritual and alchemy and magical practices are celebrated here in the holy crypt dedicated to the Virgin Mary, and we forget the churches are also places in which the Devil is given his acknowledgement and that they were built, after all, by masons.

One face of the column is given to a depiction of the

Tetramorph, a splendid beast which combines the attributes of boar, lion, donkey man and winged serpent. It is taken as the symbol of the Evangelists and of the receiving of the gospels. It possesses two tails which grow out of the body of the serpent. One of these takes the form of the fleur-de-lys, which is a symbol of the Devil. Both grow from the same stem. The beast grasps with one hand the tail of the fleur-de-lys, and with another, a spear which is aimed at a hand which attempts to bite the Devil's tail. One hand grasps onto that which is ostensibly the good, whereas the animal instincts go after the bad. The figures group themselves around a circular, anti-clockwise movement in a dance of forms, whilst the Devil's tail attempts the clockwise motion of time.

On the second face of the column Christ is shown carried on the head of St. Michael. It is the well-known message of the burden of emulating Christ, but unlike later, more saccharine renderings of the subject, the figure of Christ is shown as a mature man, rather than as an infant, with his bottom saucily exposed over St. Michael's head. His arms are outstretched and are in turn supported by those of the saint. Together their poses form the outline of the pentacle, the magical sign which is used to ward off devils, but which is also used in black magic as well as in white magic. In Christ's right hand and pointing downwards to the water is the fish, his astrological ascendant and the symbol of his miraculous powers. In his left hand is an empty vessel, which symbolises the spiritual yearning for refreshment and nourishment, as well as being the symbol for the alchemical krater, the vessel within which the transformation of the base material is carried out. This in its turn is a symbol for the cranium; a pointer to the fact that the transformation occurs within consciousness.

On the third face, the figure of Christ has been metamorphosed into that of the angry and bellowing lamb, the harbinger of the Apocalypse and the Second Coming. It shows him in another aspect; awesome and terrible, with curved horns, a gaping mouth, cloven feet and wings sprouting from each of his limbs. In his outstretched hands he holds the vessel and fish as before, but the fish now points away from the water, having made an anti-clockwise movement, and the vessel is now full. It was not possible, however, to see the fourth face of the column on this visit, since it lies on the other side of the partition, in an area which was closed off from view.

Although we looked at many other things in the Cathedral, it was the column which made the deepest impact upon the two of us. We felt the excitement and tremor of its energy when confronting these dark and problematic aspects of the figure of Christ. It was the power of the serpent which was being communicated to us; the guardian of the treasure, the radiating influence of the symbol. Elsewhere in the church, the rapidly failing light contributed to the atmosphere of intensity. The changes of level and volume, with the tunneled progression of the gloomy nave and aisles, zooming to the fan vaulting of the crossing, the steps to the Trinity Chapel and the contraction of space about the apse, provided many memorable sensations. Other thoughts were blocked out as our attention was riveted by the rich materials and carvings and the flickering luminance of the stained glass, which in the darkness appeared to be absorbing light rather than giving it out.

Four hours in the Cathedral and its precincts left us with little to say beyond the dwelling over what we had seen and Terence's forthcoming tour of the place. He was to take his puzzled students to the column and expose them to its troublesome message and the unease would be communicated to them as well. On the train I went through the guidebooks once more as Terence lay down across one of the seats and slept soundly. Occasionally I would glance up at him, noting his exhaustion, listening to his heavy breathing. He lay with his hands folded over his chest, self-contained, resisting me even in sleep. Two thirds of the way back to London, the ticket inspector provided me with an opportunity to rouse him. For a moment he sat blinking before becoming fully awake. It was, I thought, quite the most subdued day that we had ever spent together. Instead of our usual boisterous conversation and the interplay of our observations, not to mention the cutting edge of our intimacy, we were drawing in and holding out in a mood of unusual seriousness. We began talking once more as we closed in on the suburbs, about the symbols and about our interest in art history. With Terence tired, I was free to range and expostulate and talked almost without a break for the next three hours, for the remainder of the journey and over drinks in a tiny pub close to Hyde Park Corner. I was suddenly extremely energetic in my speculations about visionary artists like Blake and the alternative art history I would like to see on all those difficult aspects of the inner landscape which do not fit in with programmes and definitions. I talked on about how Christ and the Devil are both symbolised by the serpent and by the sign of the fish, and how the symbols contain both meanings and charges according to the viewpoint one approaches them with. It stimulated Terence to venture his own recollection.

"I just had a dream the other night. I can't remember very much and it wasn't very clear, but I saw this snake. It was moving slowly. It disturbed me."

"Were you afraid? Could you touch the snake?" I asked

Plate 1
Andrew Fekete as an undergraduate
at Liverpool University

Plate 2
4 November 1979 –
Abstract Composition 2

Plate 3
27 December 1979 –
Homage to Duchamp

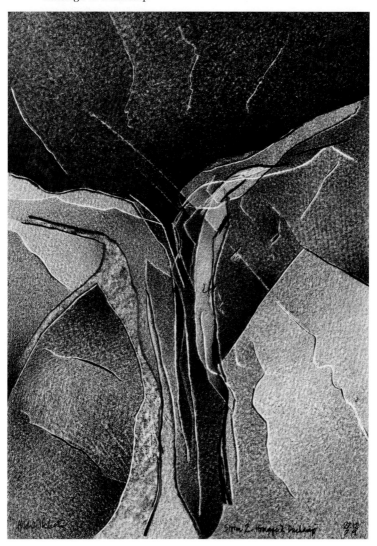

Plate 4
14 January 1980 –
The Gate to the City of the Scream

Plate 5
25 January 1980 –
The Philosophical Tree

The Fourth Face belongs to the devil....

Plate 6
21 July 1984 –
The Fourth Face Belongs to the Devil –
Diary illustration made at the time of Andrew's second
visit to Canterbury

Plate 7
2 December 1982 – Manuscript
from "The Hidden Continents" with
doodles

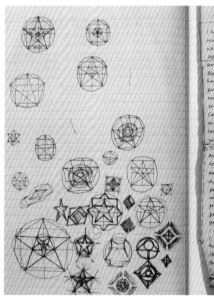

The New Gate to the gunnery

Plate 8
14 September 1979 – The New Gate
to the Gunnery

Plate 9
12 June 1982 - Active Imagination
and The Ouroboros was an Eel

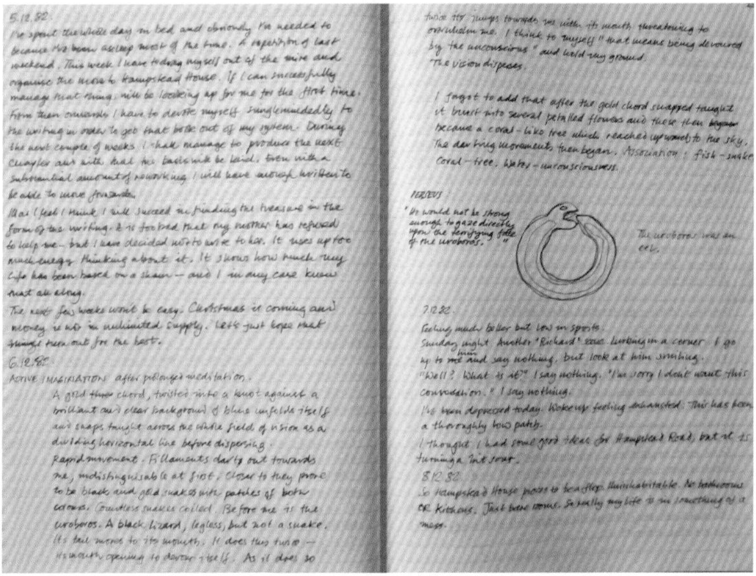

Plate 10
12 December 1982 – Shadow figure
from the diaries

Plate 11
5 August 1981 – In the Stream

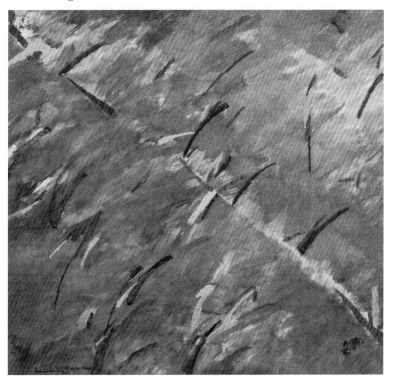

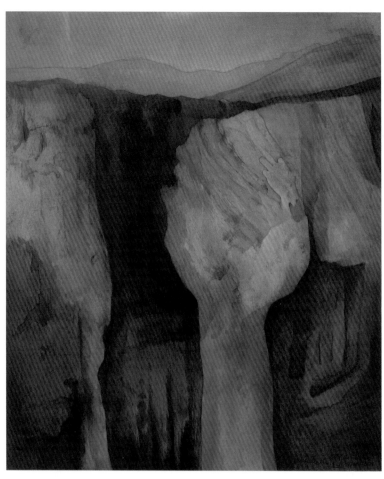

Plate 12
19 July 1981 – The Living Rock, Gotama Gate

Plate 13
Detail from The Living Rock, Gotama Gate – the image is inverted showing the Head of the Buddha suspended from an organic column.

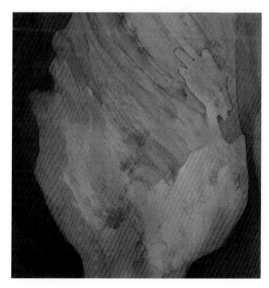

Plate 14
Detail from The Living Rock, Gotama Gate – showing
(1) the hand (top right), (2) 'Profile of agony' (top left), (3) Self-portrait (bottom middle left), (4) Other faces and images from the 'Nirvanic stream of consciousness'.

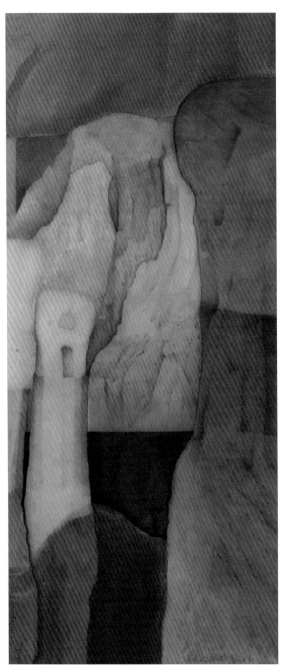

Plate 15
April 1984 –
Mysterious
Landscape

Plate 16
May 1979 - Covent Garden Piazza -
Elevation - Student project

Plate 17
May 1983 – Visionary Head
Andrew's last major painting

him.

"No. I just felt very uncomfortable and then it disappeared."

We parted company with difficulty going through the ritual of our relationship.

"We should see each other more often, away from the clubs. Please let's not meet in Subway or Heaven any more. Let's have dinner one night. You know, it's time we started treating each other with some respect."

I laughed at Terence's remark and countered.

"But stop running away from me, and maybe I'll stop running away from you as well. You're so inconsistent with me."

We were standing facing each other across the pavement and across the bicycle that Terence had ridden to the station in the morning and which he had pushed to the pub. He gave me a wry look.

"I'm a bit afraid of you. Maybe you're the serpent, my dear."

He gave me that sharp laugh of his; the one with the hint of violence in it.

I walked back through Piccadilly totally distracted and filled with excitement over the day still feeling the wave of energy which had carried me through my monologue. A pretty girl passed me and I looked back to catch what she had said to me.

"Do you want a girl for the night?"

I laughed at the incongruity of being propositioned by a female prostitute in Piccadilly. I had looked back because she didn't look like a prostitute. I said, "No thank you," but turned around again and smiled.

"Maybe next time."

I then went on to enjoy the rest of the evening, animated conversation about sado-masochism of all things, at another pub with the regulars, before finishing at the "Heaven" disco. I felt curiously out of frame, as if I was still with Terence and as if we were telepathically linked, anticipating his disturbance and wondering whether anything of the sort had really happened. I felt that he was very numbed by the day and worried about him riding his bicycle. Shutting myself off mentally from the raw sound of the music I began to feel panoramically aware, as if I could see everyone in the bar at once and could pinpoint without searching for them, where my friends were, knowing all their movements. I watched the videos and then closed my eyes, thinking, "Yes, Davidh is here too."

I saw him in my imagination standing alone, pretending not to see me, giving me the full force of his rejection of me and of my friendship. It was all a misunderstanding, I thought, and I'll prove it to him. If I change my form he won't recognise me and he will begin to be friendly with me again, reverting to the old chatter of our being mates on the town together. My ruse had worked, and to test my powers I transformed myself before him, going through my disguises. I held out the palm of my hand and three small beads glowed in its centre. They began rotating, before bursting like germinating seeds into clusters of flowers which then vanished. I had him transfixed, staring into my eyes. I touched his neck and caressed it, gradually turning him into a beautiful woman.

I felt her thighs pressing against me and held on fast, falling into darkness, losing hold. I lost consciousness.

A sharp blow to my head. I could hear a crashing noise. I couldn't remember where I was. For a moment I thought I was in my bedroom, and struggling to regain my senses I went through a list of possible causes for the pain I felt surging through my head. There is a very large painting above the bedhead and I often wonder whether it will fall off the wall and hit me. I put my hand to my head slowly and opened my eyes. I was standing at the bar and all around me I could see people talking, and I knew that because no one was looking at me that nothing had happened, but I still felt an intense aching in my head. It was then that I saw Davidh standing in front of me.

"You bastard!"

No! It was a fantasy. He couldn't have.... His reaction was incredible. The resistance....

The fourth face belongs to the Devil.

3

The Hidden Continents[1]

I had some time ago made a resolution to myself that when I was ready I would embark upon the same experiment as Ariel, which was none other than a continuation of my own venture into the realms of the psyche. Yet it was not just a desire to explore new territories which appealed to me, but the intuition that a full blooded and decisive approach would yield more than a handful of disconnected visions and would lead to a sustained and permanent shift in my consciousness. Now that I am in the midst of it I find it hard to hold on, because the disorientation is so intense. Several weeks have now passed since the visit to Canterbury stimulated me into further writing, and the passage back into "normality" has not been made. I am wandering around like a lost man in pain, acting out the automatic responses of the day without savour.

The more I thought about the Serpent and the symbols at Canterbury, the more uncomfortable I became. At moments the door moved ever so lightly to reveal unexpected twists in my interpretation and description of the vision of the serpent. I had felt satisfied with the richness of the symbols and my handling of them, but that

---

[1] This is the first version of the third chapter of *The Quest for Gold.* It exists only in handwritten manuscript form in one of the diaries.

was perhaps premature, for it is easy to dissociate oneself from them and look at them almost as a hallucination rather than as a projection of an inner psychic reality. And even when you recognise your own projections you can become complacent and open to further projections which you cannot recognise and which you perceive as external realities.

I was working late at my office and as I thought about these things, I had the distinct feeling that I was not alone in the building: a mood of paranoia, which one recognises and shrugs off. Then the doors and windows began banging. For an hour this continued, until I became so irritated by it that I had to get up and close all the windows to prevent the draught from playing any further tricks upon me, for a storm was raging outside. As I sat down again at my typewriter I listened to the rattling of the windows in their frames and the mind blowing against them from outside. The doors began banging again, loudly in an incessant rhythm. I felt exhilarated and energetic and continued with the report I was working upon, but as I sat there I froze with a vision of the corridor and the banging door, which was out of view. Running towards me was a figure, a creature over seven-feet tall with wings and a lizard's head, and with a great ruff of scales extending from its neck. I felt its presence directly opposite me and looked up in its direction; I did not feel that it was a chimera, but something very real and alive, even if it could not be perceived by the usual senses. It was demanding something from me, and I had no choice but to give it. I had to become exposed and irrational in response to this creature which had sprung up from my unconscious psyche. I had no idea what that response meant and what it had accomplished, if anything.

In 20 or 30 years' time it might be possible to make the

transition in an organised and relatively painless way, or there might exist the circumstances which could make the work possible. As a middle-aged man in his late 50s, I may perhaps receive one morning a letter from a young friend who has gone into retreat at one of the many seminaries which were set up for the induction into the work. Theodore is a conscientious ex-student of mine who still keeps in touch with his old master. I read his letter carefully and several times and meditate upon the opus before replying to him.

My dear Theodore,

I read your letter with great interest. You hold yourself in these moments with composure and good humour, and I must say that I am pleased to hear of your progress. Your work is seldom out of my thoughts and I hope that I will be able to keep myself receptive to your continued calls for advice and assistance. I know and feel that it bodes well for you and that you have cultivated the right attitude. For that reason you should follow through the steps in the correct sequence and reach the gate to the path. From then onwards the choice of response will be yours, and whatever you decide to do you will come away from the experience enriched by it. One thing, however, is missing from your background, and in this, whilst you may count yourself fortunate, I doubt whether you will truly appreciate how fortunate you are. You will experience considerable difficulties, and further shocks, of the sort you described, will await you, but throughout all this you will receive the support and encouragement of my colleagues, Demian and Susanna, and the full back-up of the community at the seminary. Now imagine, if you can, what it would be like if the Foundation had never existed and how you would manage without the Seminary and the literature of the last 50 years. Can you do that and realise how alone you would be? Oh, I know that you would give me the standard reply that we are all alone anyway, but that is only the Foundation's dogma and it isn't true for thankfully we are in these days a real community and not just individuals working alone. So even when you go to my friends and go through the sessions, try and visualise the real barren loneliness of the past and think of all those individuals who perished in the work because of that isolation. If ever you feel yourself strong, with the coming into being of the primal forces, think how much stronger they were; even those who died in harness. If you can do that you will never become complacent and will succeed where others merely mouth the truths which were experienced by others for them.

Now I know that there is very much of a romantic tendency within the whole Foundation nowadays, and I suppose a certain degree of mythology has become attached inevitably to the persons of the Archons. Remember the Founders did not chose the name for themselves, but it does convey something of the flavour of their strengths of personality and capacity for suffering and enlightenment. I was fortunate enough to have met two of them and received my induction from Alexis de Vadis. A great deal of popular literature has been written about him in particular, but the hagiographies do not come from members of the Foundation as yet, but from the laity. Somehow no one has really found the time to indulge in the luxury of biography. One reason for this is that those of us who knew him and the other Founders were impelled at the outset to eschew the cult of personality. It was they themselves who demanded that we concentrate our energies upon the work rather than look to them for salvation. This is an emphasis which is gradually being eroded, and that is why I resigned my post with the Foundation to go back to working on my own with the material itself. Hence, my reply to your letter, for I am being reminded once more of the "perils of the soul" which attend the work.

The truly remarkable thing about the achievement of the Founders in discovering the path was that the whole cultural atmosphere and ethos was inimical to their personalities and work. The times they lived in demanded that they be larger than life and supremely forceful in their personalities in order to survive against the destructive backlash of a dying culture. Please don't forget that we are still on sufferance and that the social climate still has not responded to the full challenge set up by the discovery. The only reason that the Super Powers of the main Axis tolerate the Foundation and do not wipe it out, is that the by-products of the discovery enabled them to better manage their economies and laid the foundations for real prosperity and social stability. Without sustained concentration and effort we would lose our influence, and they might perhaps feel that they could do without us. We would once more be dispersed and the literature could even be proscribed. Who knows? You might think that I am being unduly pessimistic, but I am warning you that this is indeed what lies ahead. A return to barbarism and the nihilism of the past and its persecutions. This is another reason to retain your modesty and keep a low profile about the Foundation and the Archons, especially when you go back into society. Moreover, remaining at the Seminary is in any case against the spirit of the work. It is only an expedient.

So whilst the times may appear to be ideal through the position that we hold in society I must urge you to prepare yourself for the time when the Foundation can no longer protect you or itself, for in spite of our progress, human nature remains fundamentally rooted in the animal instincts and the material world. Our philosophy will always be at variance with that position even if its influence has been a benign one.

Within the confines of the seminary you are protected from the whole range of customary interactions and responses, from envy, blank incomprehension and outright hostility and rejection. Because the atmosphere is supportive and tolerant the conflict that you experience is you own inner concern and is left for you to experience and handle. The trained personnel will, moreover, point out to you your projections so that once more their source within your adjustment of Ego will become clear to you. Without them, however, you could so easily come into conflict not with yourself, but with those around you, and thus you would become blinded to your own situation and accuse the others of it. That is still the condition of the majority outside the Foundation.

When you reach the gate a phantasmagorical world will open up to you, and under these circumstances you may lose your reality function or your hold upon material realities. Again, the Foundation will enable you to experience the experiment under controlled conditions, without these controls acting as an oppressive system. The personnel will merely steer you as you re-orientate yourself.

The Founders did not of course experience the benefits of such a system of induction and they had to carry out the work for themselves to the best of their abilities, using whatever sources were available to them, drawing largely on the work of Jung and the proto-teachings of psychoanalysis. They used such sources merely as a point of departure, and fortunately the literature was considerably developed and refined by them, for as it stood the work was only at an early stage of its development and contained conceptual flaws of such magnitude as to render it of doubtful value. That is why the early literature is now primarily of academic interest and why you are no longer required to study it. It was very much a case of obscuring the message of the path, not because the path was difficult to reach and not because the many gates to it are unyielding and refuse the penetration of consciousness, but it was simply a function of the initial resistance to the unleashing of the nuclear energies. The early pioneers were so rooted in an intellectual rationalism that they feared insanity like the plague, and because of their fear their work was always contaminated by the very thing which they could not face: their own irrationality.

So what you will now experience at the seminary is the system that the Founders developed in order to prevent this contamination of the work, so that your concentrated energies can remain pure and directed towards the Gate and the Path. But once again do not become too preoccupied with the system for that too can lead you into contamination. There are even now many worthy people within the seminary who are such perfect disciplinarians and followers of the system that they have never experienced the Gate, or but rarely. They are even trying to say that the discovery was the system and not the Gate and the Path. Approaching the Gate is something that can never be systematised. It can only be experienced.

When you study your dreams and visions forget that they have a meaning, for the search for meanings is a preoccupation of the intellect and its a priori assumptions are a primary source of contamination. One example of this is the misconception which accompanied for centuries the understanding of sacred circles and mandala symbols.

Through the intellectual preoccupation with the notion of ideal form and heavenly cosmic harmonies, the mandala was taken as a symbol of perfection and as a symbol of what man sought to find in himself. In a neurotic and unbalanced condition it is appropriate that man should seek harmony and balance within himself and the mandala with its symmetry and squaring and basis in even numbers, is an appropriate symbol for that. But at the centre of the mandala lies the hidden gold. It contains the gate to the path in a figurative and conceptual sense. It is the locus of the magical flower, the treasure, the coiled serpent and all the other symbols which denote the empowering and bursting forth of the psyche. As such the mandalas are containing symbols and concentration upon the mandala is a concentration upon the act of containment and not upon the release from it. The mandala of the crucifix contains nailed to it the serpent which demands its release. It also contains Christ.

The dreams and visions, meditations and psychic states are in themselves products of the psyche's unfolding and coming into being, in consciousness, and an increasing awareness of them leads one into a natural process of regrowth and regeneration. There are, however, occasions upon which the primal energies are gathered and projected to a point of focus and a realisation of them leads one to the many gates which open out onto the Path. These are not moments which are ordinarily accessible, because of our resistances to the psyche. One recoils from the Gate for the simple reason that it threatens or promises a change in one's condition, and just as many fear insanity, others also project upon the gate their fear of death, and there is no more powerful instinct than that. If one fears that a consequence of entering upon the gate is death itself, or a form of annihilation, that should convey the radiant, transforming energy contained at that threshold. It represents the supreme pairing of the opposing forces. If we bring to it our excessive materialism and fear of death, it follows that it contains also their opposite.

The gate is not a place but represents a unique situation or occurrence in consciousness which amounts to a shift in perception. It represents the point of transition and it is not necessarily an irrevocable or unbreachable threshold. If it were, it would not be the gate, but the path itself. So the gate is what you go through, and it follows from that that you may remain at the threshold without embarking upon the path. Such, alas, is the condition that I find myself in to this very day.

4

The Foundation[1]

I now found that I had re-embarked upon a fantastic adventure and that the sly, treacherous serpent with its dual nature provides a wonderfully apposite symbol for that. It contains within it the secret of transformation, shedding its skin and feigning death only to re-emerge in a new form. It is a harbinger of wisdom, knowledge and danger. Grasping its meaning you plunge headlong into conflict and are led down into the dirt of brothels, cheap nightclubs, dark alleyways and drug infusions; into the alchemical mire, the nighttime recess of illumination. It cannot be pinned down to a single experience or meaning, for like all symbols it contains the germ of totality. Because of that the experience of the symbol takes the form of a full-blooded assault which comes at you from all directions. It forms a circle which embraces and contains you in an ever-present womb, a cocoon of unbeing and potential being. You see it in alchemical texts as the uoroboros, the serpent which devours itself with its own teeth, or which is roasted alive to yield up the treasure it guards. And then it might make a go at you, threatening to devour you in its place. Monsters may come flying at you throughout the passage of the night, and their aim is as subtle as the madness of some black magic manifestation.

---

[1] Andrew wrote two versions of the third chapter to *The Quest for Gold*. This second version is included in a typed manuscript.

They leave you to fulfil the work yourself through your own self-destruction, through an alcoholic frenzy or through suicide. That is the dark side. It is the darkness and warmth that a weak consciousness must continue to cling to until it gains its strength through inaction and non-striving.

Imitating the process of change or inner transformation was what I had sought to achieve with Terence on our visit to Canterbury. It was also the reason for his coming to me after the break in our relationship which had occurred two years before. Ten years his junior, this was no easy task and if it ran the same course as our traumatic and turbulent relationship had done in the past the results could have been catastrophic for both of us. It could at the least have led to a very intense reaction between us. Just as had been the case with Davidh, someone closer to my own age. But as for myself it was tantamount to taking on the full flood of the psyche armed only with an immature ego striving to maintain its adulthood and masculinity.

Ariel's experience opened me to the dilemmas of a middle-aged man in the throes of a psychotic breakdown. It opened me to the essential polyvalence, the pervasive power of symbols. The effects of this ricocheted through my system like a hurricane. Without exaggeration I found myself for three months hovering on the edge of a precipice staring insanity and suicide in the face and confronting head on without any resistances, without the in-built establishment of a secure foundation in life. During complex business negotiations I had momentary respites from this strange power that was enveloping me. Pushed to the limit I could function at that executive level making multi-million pound decisions, or decisions which had that implication, but beyond the stuffed suit and pinstriped shirt I had become a creature without identity or energy. I had suffered the classic consequence of an encounter with the psyche. I was almost overwhelmed, and the struggle against the serpent which lies figuratively coiled inside us exhausted me and led to a great loss of vitality; a loss of my ability to function on a normal level.

Nevertheless, this was not my first experience of the crisis of grappling with the panoramic world of the unconscious: the inner dimension which matches the external world in microcosm for complexity and in its multifariousness. The interior landscape in its positive aspect as a territory for pioneers, heroes and explorers had already been opened up to me on countless occasions. Thus I stood face to face with the serpent in all its ranges of meaning, from the Devouring Mother to the symbol of Hermes, the bringer of enlightenment, and was fortified by my previous experiences of the symbols and by my knowledge of depth psychology. For as you are being torn asunder by the unconscious as its latent energies surge through you, you must equalise its powers to stabilise them by making less of an issue of your conscious identity and by allowing yourself to be moulded and changed by its force without losing one's humanity. With the amplification of consciousness not only do new vistas open up, but also the real nature of the world as a combination of material and biological processes with psychic ones.

One night I found myself in such a state of bewilderment that I walked twenty miles in order to exhaust myself physically. I knew, however, that no matter how distressed I became, no matter how threatened my identity was with extinction, I could neither become insane nor commit suicide. I could not flip like Ariel. Whatever pain I experienced I could not escape from it. Indeed, I had to become fully conscious of it, regardless of whatever new twist of circumstances fate had in store for me. The reason I had for this realisation was that I had experienced the psyche hitherto as an impersonal phenomenon which was not a possession of mine; as something which I had been allowed to experience and which had experienced me. No matter how difficult it may be to cope with the fear of madness, I knew that I was seeking to re-experience the realm of the spirit no longer as a momentary revelation or involuntary act of grace.

To get to it you have to go through hell. You have to abandon your fear of the serpent and make of it an ally, recognising that the primal duality consists in being simultaneously conscious and unconscious, in order to strive for a new synthesis of personality between the polar extremes, to enable the two to meet without mutual destruction is the task, and an idea of how difficult that is can be gained in an experience of telepathy, when the identities of two individuals merge. Your whole illusion of personality and reality is threatened with annihilation. If the other and I are one, what then am I? - I am an epiphenomenon, the ephemeron, the self-sustaining illusion, and so are you. It crashes upon you as a realisation which is so powerful that you must project it onto another, onto someone else. They must be evil and dangerous to threaten you with a mirror image of yourself. You hate them with an intensity that is instinctive.

I unnerve Davidh so much that he will leave a room if I am present. Even if I go up to him with a broad grin on my face and extend to him the hand of friendship, he will grimace and say to my silent communication, "I'm sorry I don't want this conversation. I must escape from you." He dares not acknowledge our mutual identity, so filled is he with self-loathing.

In fantasy I played a trick on him. Out of my conjuring hat I plucked him as if he was a creature of my own creation, dependent upon my will, and transformed him into a hermaphrodite; a being of perfection and completeness. I expressed with him my own dilemma of inner transformation, and he countered with force for force. For days I hurt from his reaction. I sought him out in order to be humiliated and rejected by him for something which was our secret and for something which no other human being could have known or thought possible. Davidh himself had no conscious idea of what had happened, and for my part I was learning very slowly. But no matter what I said to him, I could not break the deadlock between us without laying bare the illusion of personality and its identification with matter and time. To juxtapose myself in that act of will was a violation, unless responded to in equal measure.

For the year before we had mentally collided and had occupied the same space I had been psychically locked into his consciousness as if I were a demented one-function homing device. Wherever Davidh went I would follow. Returning home in the evening I would be seized by the urge to go out again, knowing where I would find him, and because of this oppressive intimacy he evaded every opportunity for friendship whilst at the same time not rejecting it. He lied about himself, his name, his personal life and career and withheld the most basic building blocks of relationship. Yet it was he who continued to encourage my self-disclosures and fantasies. I spoke to him as one who had at last found his friend, someone almost mythical and archetypal, for the friend was none other than my inner self which I had found in him. With his refusal to acknowledge me in any way, with his primitive aggression and attempts to psyche me out -

which invariably succeeded by virtue of their power - there was no longer a common ground. I too knew his secret name as son of The Mother and daughter of The Serpent. But when there was no longer any common ground between us, our relationship degenerated into an antagonistic duel in which violence was threatened with every exchanged glance. Sometimes I thought that he would kill me.

I got home very late. It was four a.m. I had just turned the key in the lock when I had the feeling that someone was standing behind me. Someone was in the corridor holding a knife. I laughed at my hyper-active imagination and made myself a mug of coffee, but the feeling of the invisible presence did not vanish with my laughter. Unable to contain my paranoia, I went out into the corridor and then down the stairs to the entrance hall. No one was there. I walked on into the street with a determined all-embracing expression on my face. The sort of expression you wear when you have to do something that you don't want to do, when you recognise its tiresome necessity.

The ancient and battered red and white Volkswagen van was there on the corner, under a street lamp, by the edge of the Common. I could not believe it. So he had come after all to kill me. I moved on to that peculiar rendezvous which we had pre-arranged. I stared at him staring at me through the windscreen, and try as I might I could not smile, because it had become deadly serious between us. ("Why? Davidh, Why?") I stepped back as he flicked on the headlights and drove on.

Several nights later I saw his van parked behind Trafalgar Square in one of the side-streets off St. Martin's Lane. I knew where he was and what he was doing, giving himself to that ecstatic abasement of a troubled consciousness, giving himself to another body in one of the fuck bars I had tried to take him out of. Away from the performance of a subtle animal, the total obsession of a prostitute on the game, giving the hide away, laying it in sacrifice to instinct, castrating one's sexuality for one's mother - castrating oneself for The Mother, yearning for the penetration of self-copulation; the mystical union. For these observations he called me a sexual fantasist, but I called back it was he.

Synchronising the moment of our meeting would not be easy, given the resistance I would have to overcome. If I met him at that ridiculous point, as he approached his van, I would have him pinned against the impossible chance occurrence with repeats itself between us in all its permutations. I walked along the Embankment, through the gardens and stared at the river and the darting lights of the illuminations shimmering across the surface of the water. I walked on to Westminster Bridge and scanned the dull blank silhouettes of the monuments against the black night sky. Ready to turn, I gave one last affectionate glance at the panorama I knew so well, the sweep of the river and the public buildings stacked up vertically along its banks. My eye stopped at the bridge. An elderly white haired man was leaning over a parapet, staring distractedly at the water. I watched him move on and once more lean on the parapet and continued to watch as he grasped it and placed his right leg on it. He looked suicidal enough. I then remembered where I had seen him.

"My God, that's my father!"

I ran directly to the spot. The man was now walking on with that recognisable arthritic gait, with his knees uncomfortably bent, but with his head held proudly erect. As I got closer I realised that although the resemblance was uncanny it was not my father. My commotion had at least given him second thoughts.

When I returned to find the van gone I did half think that what had happened was meant to keep Davidh and me from meeting. I felt that from the depths of his unconscious, or from mine, we had produced a diversion to make good his escape from me, because perhaps he would have killed me then.

If two people become locked in a drama of that intensity there is at least the possibility for one of them to realise the total absurdity of the situation and for them to withdraw their reactions. There is a point of comparison, and a sense of the other as being the other, with their own experiences, memories, sensations and reflexes. With the increasing self-consciousness there arises the possibility of no longer acting out the instinctive patterns of behaviour. One can through an act of will break the mould and come to realise a higher form of independence within a single relationship. But the same duel between the antagonists occurs within one's personality, between the polarities of consciousness and the unconscious, and because of the interior nature of this struggle it is much harder to locate it and become aware of it. The precious personality and ego which you have cultivated for so long are layered over another who is also struggling for expression and an outward form in its coming-into-being. You harbour this other as if it were a dangerous parasite which threatens to overwhelm the thing one fought so hard to attain: the conscious personality.

Four years ago I would not have taken such an intense view of the nature of consciousness. My outlook was wholly and decidedly intellectual and the non-intellectual aspects of my personality and behaviour occurred in another continuum unrelated to me.

Many experiences laid down for me the foundations for my dealings with this other being. They were not isolated outbursts of another consciousness, but rather peaks in a continuous process which originated in the prehistory of my childhood, when dark rooms and nights brought to me luxuriant visions - ecstatic visions and the luxuriant enjoyment of participation. I read that children are rooted in the unconscious and that the development of Ego is the wresting of consciousness from its primal embrace, but I was a peculiarly conscious child with adult fantasies and preoccupations, being brought up in a household surrounded by adults. I re-experienced the suddenness of my death by an almighty blow across my head and leaped back into consciousness and life with a jerk in sharp reaction to that endless falling into the void. Lights glowed in my room, patterns collided with the walls and the ceiling opened up into an infinity of changing vistas, colourful forms, abstract dimensions, which enveloped me as I lay on my bed sinking into sleep. The memory of that original experience was so vivid and remarkable that it never left me. When the cleavage arose and the visions came to me no longer I knew that I had lost something of tremendous value and something which I would spend the rest of my life trying to recover. Occasionally glimpses of it came to me if I closed my eyes too tight, but it was never the same. It was a fraudulent gimmick by comparison.

As an artist I attempted to rediscover that first landscape within the medium of my compositions. At first I defined my search as one for the fourth dimension. Through a sheer elaboration of forms I sought to puncture the pictorial screen and shatter it so that it could no longer be taken as art in the strict referential sense, so that a painting would become a world of its own, suggestive of its own laws. Adolescent friends remarked that these paintings reminded them of their acid trips and that they felt as if they could walk into them and go on exploring their territory beyond what they could see in the picture plane. And this is what I intended, but it did not take me long to discover that if there was a fourth dimension it lay within me and that I had no need to seek it elsewhere. But the dream of the fourth dimension became another reality as it was overtaken by the fantasy of creating an image so real that you could disappear into it forever. That too was Herman Hesse's dream, and knowing that made me realise that the missing dimension lay within me, and that there was no need to seek it elsewhere.

Absentmindedly I always drew little scribbles in notebooks, elaborate doodles which were given little conscious thought, but which on later inspection proved to be beautifully ordered. Then I began to base my paintings on these and abandoned the rules of composition as an act of imposition. The paintings acquired a new life, intensity, brooding and depth. People found them disturbing, but could not say why. They were abstract, but they were not purely formal. They now had content and presence.

I had completed a series of monochrome drawings in this manner when late one night I succumbed to an abscess on a tooth. To take my mind off the intense pain, I sat down in a corner of my flat in an armchair and painstakingly drew in pencil on a sheet of paper a dull grey background. I carried on the shading through the whole night automatically and mindlessly, simply allowing my hand to move randomly across the sheet producing finely grained textures and dots. It was not a promising start.

When I finished the drawing into which I also introduced a line to divide the composition into two halves, I began to notice forms emerging from the shading. The drawing which had been so obsessively worked upon came to life. Everywhere I looked its surface was crammed with the faces of individuals from different historical epochs. Renaissance courtiers, Mayan princes, medieval grotesques, stately Roman profiles and contemporary figures, all of them carefully and precisely delineated in styles appropriate to their period, in styles of rendering in which I had had no training other than with my eye as a student of art history. Then the figures became more animated. They merged into a torrential flow of forms. Faces contained faces overlaid upon each other and there was movement. The drawing constellated new delights for me as I entered into its happy hallucinations. Herman Hesse stood smiling benignly in one corner opposite a self-portrait of myself, advancing in years. A Jesuit priest was at prayer, a Buddhist monk in deep contemplation. A man and a woman were locked in embrace. To this day, the figures of the Nirvanic Stream are there, encapsulated in the drawing which taught me that its world is at all times visible to those who can see it.

To say this world is produced from the depths of the unconscious is not a very satisfactory answer, because that reduces it simply to a formulation. What kind of thing is the unconscious if we can produce from it spontaneous images of things which burst upon one in so unexpected a manner? I did not, however, have any doubt that I had caught reality unawares, or my own consciousness was in abeyance and the curtain had parted; the impenetrable barrier had now shifted, and my questions were beginning to be answered from another world which we can conveniently call the psyche. I also found that I could do things which I could not do before. I could paint landscapes of mountains and ravines, Alpine scenes, icy flows, misty Japanese ridges and volcanoes, where previously I had had no knowledge of rock formations and their overlooking skies. My psyche was opening up to me and if I could not as yet possess its visions in an unalloyed form I could at least project them and materialise them with my paint brushes.

From the universal impersonal of the Nirvanic Stream I became excited by Buddha's example; the transcendental possibility he opened up to mankind. I wanted to pay homage to him, the first foundation stone of our modern spiritual culture; he who is so deeply embedded and engrained into every form and organism of our planet, dissipated, but all-present. I had seen photographs of the statues of Buddha which have been carved into cliff faces and mountains throughout Asia. These monuments seemed to me to be at variance with the impersonal nature of the Buddhist canon. I did not realise then that they act as vortices for the Buddha's universal presence.

I decided that I would attempt to convey my excitement through painting a portrait of Buddha, using a photograph of one of these statues as my source. I knew something was up. I was drinking in a pub with some friends when I was seized by the expectation that something exciting was about to happen. I said that I was going to paint the portrait of Buddha and rushed home to do so. As I worked, the painting painted itself in a manner which no longer surprised me. I allowed my concentration to rest in the details and did not concern myself with the composition which grew organically. I would paint a smear or smudge of brilliant colour and then blot it with tissue paper and gradually build up forms from the leftover traces of colour. The individual parts of the rocky scene I had discovered in the painting fascinated me so much that I completely forgot and abandoned my original theme. There was the base of a ravine which I spent hours carefully outlining, drawing with my finest brush in miniature detail. Tiny paths led up perilous rocks, twisting to avoid the sudden turns and drops of the landscape. When I had filled in the last patch of the palest blue sky I felt the painting was finished. All the surfaces had been worked upon, reworked and had had many layers of different colours applied to them with the thinnest of washes. I was ready for my favourite ritual, to pin the painting to a wall and to re-enter it as a spectator.

Cellular creatures, hands grasping the living rock, the profile of an Aztec man gazing serenely at a column which surged out of the cliff face. An antique lady in a splendid headdress placed next to a Buddhist monk.

The column itself was originally going to support the standing figure of Buddha, but early on in the effort I realised that it was not something that I would be capable of pulling off. I merely left an outline, a suggestion of where Buddha might be. I then took another look. Yes, a curious shape was embedded in the column. I could not quite make it out, but when I looked at it again I could see it clearly. I had not noticed it, because I had not expected to see a hand there. The apparition pleased me no end, for the drawing of hands is a test of skill which usually eludes me. There it was, perfectly formed and pointing in the direction of the sky, giving the gesture which marks the completion of the alchemical opus. It almost seemed to be moving. As I concentrated on it the foreground of rocky forms seemed to be merging with the distant ridges beyond them. The whole composition seemed to be gathering in momentum, rushing upwards towards the hand, as if everything had now become focused upon it. It was then that it came out of the painting and pointed at me and back again to the sky in a circular movement which was repeated several times. Exhilaration and elation overtook me as I felt myself rushing to meet that patch of sky illuminating the most distant of the mountainous ridges. I had stumbled upon something momentous, laughing and crying like a confused child, resisting its attraction only out of cowardice.

I had experienced the foundation as a force which had opened up to me a revelation of transpersonal values in such a manner as to stress their impersonal character. These values are not a possession of the ego, but of the psyche. Wherever and whenever the ego attempts to manipulate the psyche it ceases to be that benign force which brings with it insight and wisdom and on the contrary it unleashes its destructive potential, for it is bipolar in nature. It is the original unity, the Tao, the hermaphrodite, the Atman. They represent the union of heaven and earth as the original unity which existed before consciousness came along and divided them, where spirit and matter are inseparable and are intertwined, just as are heaven and hell. Failing to perceive this you reach up to heaven and find yourself in hell, for the ego cleaves to opposites and carries with it an innate tendency to particularise in its isolating focus. The hound grasps the serpent's tail and finds itself with the Devil. It becomes peculiarly immured in darkness and chaos, out of its very strivings for order.

*

Since ego-consciousness cleaves to opposites and differentiates between opposing concepts and distinguishes in its mastery of perspective between the foreground and the background, between heaven and earth, it is forever shifting in its focus; particularising and isolating. Thus it carries with it an innate tendency to inflate one particular object or aspect of reality above all others. It cannot in itself contain totality, and how can it? It is a creature of relativity, built up out of the recognition of viewpoints, from acts of comparison and the growing sense of its isolation and separation from the world around it. As an orientating device it serves its purpose. It sets coordinates, knows the locus, and is forever going somewhere from something behind it which has been experienced, passed over or superseded. Yet the ego possesses an intimation of something else which lies behind the veil of reality. In its dreams and fantasies it can fly and do miraculous things, it can read the thoughts of others and burrow down to their deepest secrets. At least it thinks it can. Its prevalent myth is that of the Superman when it associates its endeavours with those of the Superman.

The Superman is unique because he is the possessor of power; he is charged with the energy which surges through him. This is energy which radiates from him to his surrounding environment along a natural gradient. It passes from him to those who do not possess it, and they too become empowered and capable of doing anything whilst under his motivation. But he is nothing without moral authority and discrimination. He is then no longer the possessor, but the possessed: a madman we may lock up or a madman we elect to power. He is dangerous precisely because he has power, too much of it for his tiny ego and personality to contain.

Identifying with the psyche we run the risk of thinking that we too can possess its powers. To a limited extent we can experience them, and that participation in itself encourages us in our belief that we have been the creators of the power. This is where artists are fortunate in knowing the difference between creative inspiration and those fallow periods in which pages are torn up in disgust, paintings slashed, or worse still when the masterpiece one laboured over is a flop. They project upon a work their own inner opus, and can experience its transformation before their eyes. It unfolds of its own inner logic and becomes reified - transmuted into matter. It stands before you as an object wrested from the domain of the psyche, for further reflection and inspiration. Thus when you have a work to work upon you also objectify the psyche, and experience it as an objective reality.

Thus the foundation is also an awareness of the other as the other and not as oneself. It is inexplicable and not of the human realm and must retain its mysteries. When you experience it as this unfathomable, but nonetheless objective quality that fortifies you in the almighty struggle with illusion which comes with the nigredo, the black night of the soul. Possessing this knowledge that it is complete in itself and not of your creation you learn to unravel the bathos of your own unreality and by stages come into greater being.

The foundation is also in a real sense a community of individuals which is being formed out of the social crisis of the present. Individuals who are learning to break the instinctual mould of their projections, their desires, and their need for certainty and leadership. They are mutants in the eyes of the old collective order. Indeed their consciousness is a mutation which is dictated by the demands of evolution. Upon their success and failure, their ability to contain themselves without capitulating to psychotic ideals or frenzies, depends the fate of our global experiment.

In some form or another I spent the last ten years searching for The Foundation. I began by projecting it onto the society I found myself in, and to this day I do not understand why it has proved to be so elusive a search.

Perhaps I was naive, but I expected to find it in a great city like London. I still haven't found it other than in the form of my relationships and in my creative work or whatever is created within myself. I am forced to conclude therefore that it doesn't exist here. This is not the right soil for it. This anti-cultural city that I know so well. The anti-city of scattered individuals - the city of isolated communities, classes and ethnic groups which seldom interact positively. London society is hermetically sealed, insular and parochial despite its dazzling array of meaningless opportunities. It is the devouring city in its negative sense. It swallows up individual destinies and careers and reduces them. It is a city without a core, without a life on the street, without boulevards and coffee houses. A place of sectarian interests and cliques.

But this year I became a courtier to a multi-national company and suddenly found myself pirouetting and being lionised by a small section of London society. I discovered that its clandestine operations are rather like those of the Freemasons and the Mafia. You are invited to join it and the invitation is couched in such a way that you cannot refuse, because you have already been marked apart as a part of it. What a flattering illusion. Doors open where they were firmly shut. At smart dinner parties where you have heard of everyone present or read about them, you are introduced to so and so, and over the salmon starter it dawns on you that she doesn't know who you are, but assumes automatically that she ought to. She is an eminent and elderly magazine editor, influential and amusing. You are the reticent resident poet or artist and have become fashionable. For a couple of days I am pestered over the phone for trivial bits and pieces of information: a transparent pretext, until I drop the matter, even though I like the woman.

*

Meeting Ariel again for the first conversation since the autumn was something that I had looked forward to for some time. Anticipating ahead of the event I felt that he might still have some surprises up his sleeve, but pinning him down to a definite meeting was not the easiest of tasks. To forewarn myself I took the precaution of ringing Vasilis to enquire as to Ariel's present health and state of mind under the pretext of having lost his telephone number. Vasilis too proved to have been through a difficult time. Over the phone he catalogued his disasters.

"But God, have I had problems myself!"

I asked him why he had moved from his studio.

"Well, I've gone bankrupt! I've lost everything. There is no point in my doing anything at the moment, so I'm just sitting here in this tiny bedsit thinking of ways not to go mad. I can't work, because whatever I earn they take away from me, so there's no point. I'm better off on the dole."

It was a familiar story and one which I myself had only narrowly avoided twelve months ago. "How much have you gone down for, Vasilis?" I asked.

"£7,000 my dear. It makes me sick just thinking about it. I put everything, my own money, and borrowed money as well, into an exhibition. The catalogues were printed, the invitations were sent out and the gallery just went bust, and I didn't have enough time to arrange anything else. Anyway, I still have my paintings, which is something, even though I haven't got room for anything else other than myself. At the moment I can't paint. It's disgusting."

Vasilis gave me Ariel's telephone number and his regards to pass onto him and invited me to visit him, providing I would bring some champagne to help him think of better times. This I promised to do. Failing, however, to contact Ariel whose line was constantly engaged, I got together for dinner that evening with my ex-tutor instead.

Doug and I sat in a tiny little Italian restaurant after our rendezvous in Tottenham Court Road and engaged each other in a tangential conversation about our respective architectural interests and a minor government scandal that we're both indirectly involved in. We went over the angles of the article he was going to write about it making comments that we could not repeat elsewhere and gauging each other's motivations. It all seemed like a storm in a kettle, nothing but steam rising to meet the cold air of a January evening.

Casually he reached over to the wine bottle and told me about his divorce and about the prospect of bankruptcy without any work coming in and how his left eye got burnt to a frazzle whilst fixing the spotlights for an exhibition at his college.

"Since I've lost my eye I've been following this subject, and do you know that every time there's an eclipse in India, 60,000 people go blind just through looking at the sun?"

He gave me a cool anatomical description of how the eye becomes scarred through focusing on an intense source of light. A description which made me feel extremely uncomfortable; uncomfortable on just about every level.

"Did you realise that the eye is a part of the brain?" he asked. "It's actually attached to the brain. It's not just an organ, but a part of how you judge and perceive the world."

His story reminded me of Davidh's experience with the serpent. I could now appreciate it not simply as an intellectual idea or as a subject for analysis, but as a physical reality or sensation. I had been meditating one evening after reading some passages on yoga when my imagination ranged over Davidh's acid experience. I remembered that there is a certain wormlike parasite which can be picked up through the skin and which travels through the bloodstream until it reaches the brain. Just as the tapeworm makes itself comfortable in the intestine, this particular creature chooses the brain as its gruesome supper dish and habitation. From that gory piece of medical gossip it takes little imagination to actually feel the presence of something alien under your scalp, to feel the presence of an unwelcome guest interfering with your consciousness and bodily functions. Escalating the fantasy and experiencing it under the influence of hallucinatory drugs takes it into the realm of graphic and bloody horror.

Every time I tried to reach Ariel on the phone over the next few days he proved to be unavailable. "I'm sorry I've got to see my mother today. I always see her on a Sunday."

Or else he would tell me that he has had to have an urgent meeting with his financial advisers. Inverting our roles with each other, I told him.

"I want to see you Ariel. I must see you now that my diary is free."

"Are you still working so hard with your buildings?" he asked me.

I explained to him that I was in the throes of giving birth to 100,000 square feet of them.

"My word, that is a labour," he exclaimed. "You must have a very capacious womb. I will have to inspect such a womb, it must be quite remarkable."

We talked on in that vein, but without fixing anything up. "Ring me tomorrow," he said. "I might be free then."

With a Sunday on my hands and with Ariel visiting his mother, I in turn visited John. He answered the front door dressed only in a dirty white t-shirt. I saw him approaching me through the frosted glass of the door, or rather I was more aware of a smudge of pubic hair approaching me through the frosted glass, and a bared behind darting back into his room. Once inside, he explained himself.

"I knew that I could answer the door like this, because you pressed the doorbell under the window sill. Only close friends know where that bell is. It's my security system against the rent collector and the gasman."

Watching him slide into his jeans I picked my way through the debris on the floor and cleared a space to sit on. It turned out to be his cutting board. Apart from the general profusion of different types of cloth, leather, sheets of copper and silver which were going to be worked into jackets as applique panels, the most striking new feature of his ever-changing and chaotic living space was a series of newspaper headlines stuck to the wall next to the mantelpiece; all of them culled from *The Evening Standard*. Together they made an elegant and amusing elegy for the whole fiasco of the Falklands War:-

GOOD
NEWS
ALL
ROUND

HOME
ARE
THE
FALLEN

113

HOW
COULD
IT
HAPPEN?

SONG
OF
SURVIVAL
PARADISE

"If you just wait for me to finish getting dressed I'll make us some tea and then you can tell me your news whilst I make up this pattern."

It did not take him long to re-emerge from the even more striking debris of his kitchen with a steaming kettle and a pair of suspiciously stained mugs. After lighting an ancient paraffin heater and placing the kettle on it to avoid having to boil up more water he lit up some cannabis resin and began the day with a gasp of the acrid fumes which had collected in a clear glass tumbler.

"I'm waiting for some more of this stuff. My junky friend is coming round later on with it. I've managed to persuade him now to get off heroin, but unfortunately he's not as interesting now that he's off it. I enjoyed playing with him before. Anyway, how are you getting on with the writing? Is it getting on with you yet?"

Recalling my recent experiences provoked him into a monologue about his sexual adventures, which were by now familiar to me and no longer even listened to sceptically.

"You know when you've had a really good fuck you're totally out of it, and the more you don't think about anything at all, the better it is? It's the orgasm living through you. When that happens that's like a Zen experience. And then you start to enter into the mind of the other person as well and start reading their thoughts, and they start reading yours. Afterwards you find yourself answering a question they haven't asked. You get funny jumps in the conversation, hey? Well, if you take that further you start to use the whole thing creatively to begin leap frogging your own consciousness. When I do that I start to feel I've located the hidden woman in me, and you know what that means don't you? It was like that when I was having my sister."

Not wishing to be regaled again on the subject of his incestuous childhood, I cut him short.

"I think that means you're a spiritual whore. '"

"Yes! Oh yes! But aren't you one as well? You're always so uptight about it, but I've got one thing for you to think of. In Tantric sex the whole purpose is to use your partner to locate the opposite within yourself, for a man to find his female side and for a woman to find her male side. That's why the men also shaved all their body hair off. When you do that you realise that all sex is just an attitude of mind. The masculine and the feminine are purely a matter of how you happen to feel. They're there within you and waiting for you to find them."

Laughing at the idea I told him, "I think I would just find all that too embarrassing, John."

As we talked, John continued with his work, spreading the pattern cloth on the carpet and using the floor as his ironing board. Looking around I noticed the pack of tarot cards on the mantelpiece and remarked,

"These have become very tatty all of a sudden. I thought they were a new set."

He looked up nonchalantly.

"Oh they've become very worn. Would you do me a favour and shuffle them?"

I felt that he was up to something and picked them up reluctantly, and with quite some resistance shook them about and rearranged them. John watched my discomfort with a triumphant grim.

"I knew you would feel like that. That's Philip's set. He's done hundreds of readings with them and I took them away from him because they'd got into such a bad state."

"I'm not surprised," I replied. "They're giving off a dreadful vibe."

"Oh yes, but they'll be better soon. You've given them a push in the right direction."

With the rest of the day ahead of me, I decided to spend my time at the Victoria and Albert Museum, deciding to go there on the off chance of discovering whether or not it had any Romanesque carvings to match those at Canterbury. However, after my conversation with John I was not very surprised to bump into Philip in the middle of the Brompton Road as I crossed over to reach the Museum. We met on the traffic island and had our first non-hostile exchange on the subject of his worn-out tarot pack.

"John just came along and took them away from me and gave me his instead. I'm quite glad really. People only come for a reading because they've got problems and want to hear an answer. The cards just absorb their karma and they were beginning to get very sticky with it."

Inside the Museum it took me quite some time to find out what I had made the journey for. I looked around indifferently at the Renaissance treasures which I had known since my childhood, remembering what Terence had said about the only sculptural work there by Michelangelo. There is a tiny sketch in clay of a dying slave, a working model for his famous unfinished marble. It's the sort of piece that you can very easily overlook, not realising its importance. I gave it a cursory glance, amused by the fact that Terence had tried to catch me out with it by testing my knowledge. Like most of the tourists I was looking at the objects cramming the display cases without really looking at them, and passing the great set-pieces indulgently, as if I was flicking through the pages of a favourite but somewhat over-familiar book.

The Museum is a fantastic agglomeration of piled up loot which still reflects the tastes of the great Victorian collectors and the pickings from the exhibitions, not all of them in good taste. One newly opened gallery attracted me because it was devoted entirely to a display of faked treasures, appropriately located next to the Cast Court and dominated by a replica plaster cast of Trajan's Column comically positioned in two sections, because cavernous as the Court is it still cannot accommodate the column in one piece. The catholicism of the Museum's tastes and didactic purpose is illustrated by these fakes and replicas. Looking at them you forget that they aren't the originals, in spite of the curious juxtapositions between them. The portal of Santiago de Compostela, the Puerta de la Gloria, is jostled by a crush of carvings and sculptures. It's like a badly digested art history book in which the pages have been shuffled about and in which nothing quite fits together. One embarks upon a crazy Grand Tour which races across Europe in a couple of hours.

A Canadian tourist, obviously impressed by the profusion of objects, came up to me and asked,

"Are these for real?"

When I explained to him that they were not he found that even more remarkable.

"You mean that column is made out of plaster? How does it stand up?"

Escaping from him I settled on hunting out carvings

from the same period as those in the Undercroft at Canterbury Cathedral, but sadly none of them came up to the same level of intensity. The casts taken from the Norwegian wooden churches, from Hallingdal and Urnes, did however come close with their strikingly pagan symbolism. Their interlocking swirls of foliage produce a finely laced screen of decoration which conceals snakes and dragons and attenuated stags on impossibly spindly hind legs, reaching up to nibble at tendrils which loop over them. These are all rich symbols of the ouroboric serpent which simultaneously devours and regenerates itself.

From the church of St. Sebaldus in Nuremberg there is a cast of the Schreyer-Landauer Monument of Christ bearing the Cross, the Crucifixion and Entombment and the Resurrection, carved by Adam Kraft. The mason's name is almost a riddle. The mason Adam carved a Monument to the Son of Adam and lavished superb skill and care in the depiction of his suffering and horrible wounds, and the mocking faces of his tormentors and the grieving of his followers.

The Cross on Calgary is itself a riddle, because it lacks the top most arm and forms a "T". You might think that the mason had carved the fourth arm and that it had broken off, but in another form it is the alchemist's "Y", the symbol of hermaphroditism, the reconciliation of duality through the redemption of the original man.

My disjointed day terminated with drinking at The Salisbury on St. Martin's Lane. I found myself shifting about, unable to suppress my boredom, and was just about to leave when I noticed that there was a champagne bucket next to me, in which there was a single bottle of Moet. Turning around I found myself in the company of an acquaintance. Only an exiled Armenian millionaire would stand there drinking champagne in a pub on his own. I ribbed him about his extravagance.

"I'm anti-social," he said. "I like being on my own. I don't like affairs. I don't like being married, so I stand here drinking champagne to pick up young boys. Sometimes they're interesting and sometimes they're pretty."

I left him to the pretty boys who were standing around him and communicated the news to Derek, David and Alistair who had just arrived.

"Where? Where is he?" demanded Derek. "He's just right for David. He can have him and I'll have the money! We'll do a deal on it."

They went off searching for the Armenian millionaire, thinking that he must be in another part of the bar and not realising that he was standing behind me and sharing the joke I was having at their expense; smiling cynically in our direction.

Derek began to make the charade more obvious.

"Oh you can't do this to us! You must tell us where he is."

I stepped back and pulled a glass of beer over myself, thinking, "It's getting to me."

"I'm reading this, and I can't read anything without experiencing it as well," I said to Derek, pointing at the thick volume of Jung's *Mysterium Coniunctionis* that I was carrying.

"That's wonderful!"

He picked the book up and showed me the Riddle of Bologna.

"Do you realise that's what my films are about? Few people know that."

I began to reel with drink. I was beginning to understand what I was doing to myself.

On Monday afternoon Ariel and I finally chose the National Portrait Gallery as the locale for our meeting. I spent the morning buying books and arrived laden with them five minutes early at 3.25. The warm foyer with its comfortable leather chairs proved to be a sensible place to wait for him, but just as I had settled down and was beginning to look over my books he came through the glass swing doors.

"Let's get out of this place. It gives me the willies."

He grabbed my arm and pushed me towards the door.

"Why Ariel? This is a wonderful building."

Looking irritable and tired he explained.

"It may be a lovely building my dear, but the paintings are not. Just looking at them gives me a headache. Now let's go."

We walked rapidly towards Leicester Square looking for a coffee bar in which we could sit and talk. Asking to see which books I had bought, Ariel was particularly interested in one by Marie Louise von Franz on the theme of Redemption.

"Do you know, my analyst was trained by her? He went to Switzerland to study with her in the '50s."

Finding a suitable coffee bar proved to be a less than straightforward task. I wanted to go to the Swiss Centre, but that was closed, and I positively vetoed Ariel's suggestion of Akram's Bar.

"It's just too uncomfortable there." I said. "And anyway Akram is no longer running it. He's retired. I think he made so much money from all his kebab places that he's now trying to turn kosher, and that for an Arab is not an easy task."

"He was always very nice to me," Ariel lamented.

"That's all very well, but he beat up his staff."

I was getting annoyed, and out of the lack of anything better we had to make do with the Tennessee Pancake House, the sort of place that's filled with down-at-heel waiters who take out their resentment at the management on their customers. Waiting for our coffees, both of us looked flyblown after being in the wind. I wanted to tell Ariel that I had written about him, but the fact that his present attitude seemed so matter-of-fact made it difficult for me to begin what I wanted to say.

"I was very moved by what you were going through. Do you remember that?"

Ariel looked at me through his National Health specs as if I had said something unwelcome.

"I could not say very much about it, because I did not understand what you were doing, but you had painted some pictures of the Philosophical Tree which I felt were very important. You were very funny, throwing rice about, saying that you were going to plant trees, and very loveable as well."

Ariel gave me his best angelic smile.

"Oh I am always very loveable. Yes, it was all very strange. Do you know what it was? Well, I didn't know either. It kept on happening to me that I would go through these states, and then my doctor discovered that there's an imbalance in my metabolism which makes me lose control over things. At the time it's wonderful, but afterwards I get very depressed. It's all caused by a lack of salt in my system. I was taking drugs for it, but they got the mixture wrong. They were testing a new drug with me and it actually made things worse."

I wasn't quite sure how seriously I could take Ariel's story. He was looking at me in a testing, probing sort of way which made me feel uncomfortable and foolish.

"Don't get me wrong though. It's no ordinary salt. It isn't sodium chloride, but a very, very special salt. Without it I can't fix things. I can't make sense of my experiences. That's what I mean. Without this salt it's hell."

"I think I understand," I said. "Salt preserves things and prevents them from going off, from putrefying. You need to take things with a pinch of salt."

Ariel lit up a cigarette and offered me one before continuing.

"Exactly. In New York I have a friend who rings me up from time to time and he has the same experiences. He doesn't have this salt either. To compensate for it I'm now on lithium. It's helping me, but it doesn't make it any easier for me to live in this terrible world. You know, I look around at these young kids today, as they're taking drugs, and I think, 'Poor bastards'. They've just got to escape from it all, into something like drugs or sex. I feel really sorry for them, because inside them they've got something really wonderful.

Well, I got very worried about it, because I thought that it was because of the poppers I was taking for sex, but it wasn't that. I stopped using it, but it didn't make any difference. It all came back to this salt."

Ariel's attitude confused me, and I hoped that I could stimulate him into a more forthright admission of his experiences by describing my own experiments.

"I don't like taking drugs, because I find that I can have the same experiences without them. Perhaps they're not as striking as the things that people go through when they're on acid, but when they happen I'm fully conscious of them. I am aware of what's going on and don't just write it off as something caused by a drug. I know that I am the source of the interference, or something in me is. That makes a tremendous difference, because then I go away and work out what it actually means. If you've seen Buddha, for instance, that's something very obscure, and at the same time it's the most important thing that can happen to you. It stands apart from everything else. You find the treasure, but then you've got to find out what it's for. It doesn't just begin and end with the experience, it's constantly changing, moving on, and it's very demanding, because you've got to have nerves of steel to be able to cope with it."

Ariel was somewhat taken aback by my earnestness.

"Last time we talked you were going to become a millionaire, a Buddhist millionaire. Your attitude seems to have changed a bit, hasn't it?"

"Well, I've gone through something as well. It's something a lot of people are going through. It's in the atmosphere. People are living under the shadow of the bomb and some of us aren't just sitting around waiting for it to happen, but are working fucking hard on ourselves to make sure that if it does it won't matter. With my work I'm just a courtier at a multinational, and artist who's turned businessman. I certainly don't take what I say about it seriously. Like you I also talk about things metaphorically, but some people don't notice. They take it literally. But the problem sometimes arises when I've been tripping on my own inner juices, and the next day I've got to be at the negotiating table. That puts me on the spot. Some days I've felt suicidal. I've felt the Devil beside me making a go at me, and then at the same time I'm boarding a plane for a meeting in another city. I can't afford to go down with it. Not the plane, the Devil!"

"Well that sounds very exciting," Ariel commented. "I hope you're making a lot of money out of it, and when you do become a millionaire you will invite me to your villa in the South of France."

Ariel was becoming restless.

"You know, I just can't understand it. There's so much unhappiness around at the moment with this Depression. Do you think it will get better? - My mother lives in a big block in St. John's Wood - that in itself is unimportant - and she lives alone, surrounded by other people. Things are getting quite difficult for her, because she's 79 now. But do you think anyone of those fine people ever care to see how she is or ask if she needs anything? My sister visits her for an hour every Tuesday, and apart from that and my spending my Sundays with her, she has no other human contact. And I'm talking about a good woman. A fine woman who has done a lot for other people. That's how they treat a good woman.

"Now I think we had better finish our coffee and go for a walk. Let's look at the sunset. I think you'll find that it is quite special."

We walked on through Piccadilly and up Regent's Street against the tide of the rush-hour commuters. It was five o' clock and the expensive shops that we passed and stared into were deserted in spite of the attractions offered by the January Sales. One shop seemed at variance, however, with the respectable elegance of the street. It specialised in work overalls and uniforms. A nurse's outfit caught Ariel's fancy.

"That's my new costume, definitely! I shall buy that for a drag ball that Tulip and I are going to. What do you think? Don't you think I will look wonderful as a nurse?"

Looking at diamond tiaras and jeweled watches in the windows of Mappin & Webb provided another surreal contrast.

"Not a customer."

Ariel's comment was overheard by a shop-assistant who looked up anxiously, as if reminded of the threat of redundancy.

"Look, it's absolutely deserted. Dead. And they say that the economy is picking up. Shall I buy you a tiara? Shall we do our bit to end the recession? Or perhaps you'll buy me one when you become a millionaire."

Ariel was by now limping and began to clutch at my arm as we walked on slowly towards Oxford Circus. The books I held onto in my other arm kept slipping, and so every few hundred feet I had to stop and readjust them. Eventually I had to let go of Ariel and leave him to limp on unaided.

"What a splendid sky," he said, pointing towards a gap in the buildings and a gash of deep violet.

"Do you think that any of this will survive when they press those buttons? I used to be very naive about it, thinking that it was all part of a grand design that we couldn't understand, but which somehow made sense. Now I think it's just senseless. Just look at that sky. There may be other worlds there, if we can look hard enough for them. Those worlds might be all around us. What do you think? Do you believe in other worlds?"

"Of course I do. Now let's step out."

We eventually parted company at Regent's Park Underground Station, after walking up past the Adam and Nash terraces of Portland Place and after I had pointed out to him the buildings along the route. We agreed that we would meet again as soon as I had finished my move to a new flat closer to the centre of town. I left him with conflicting impressions, feeling that whatever was going on with him was not quite connected up. There was a rich undercurrent which I could feel, but which left him untouched. Or perhaps he knew more than he was letting onto. His parting remark I took as an ironic comment on our afternoon together.

"Thank you for enlightening me."

On the journey home I began to doodle in my notebook, deep in thought about the conversation with Ariel which had left me feeling depressed. I flicked past other doodles and started to compare them. There were familiar mandalas, squared circles which were based on the symmetry of the cross. There were intricate geometric and structural doodles and free form curvilinear ones. The mandalas, I had read, mean differentiation, balance and centering; the striving for a harmonic order. The curved ones, however, link themselves into dancing copulating pairs. There was a whole page of them jumping about telling me of an unconscious drive towards conjunction, towards the mystical union of opposites. And then I flicked back to an inelegant and crude drawing I had made of the ouroboric serpent. It had become so ubiquitous a symbol to me that I almost ignored it, but on glancing back I found that I had drawn something in its centre. The serpent formed a circle, but within it there was a facetted jewel. I looked at it again.

"But of course. That's the treasure"

The treasure is contained within the ouroboros, within the unconscious. That is why it is so hard to find. It has to be yielded up by the unconscious in a purely voluntary fashion, and no amount of conscious concentration or meditation will achieve that. Indeed the harder you concentrate on it the further away from the treasure you are, for within the concentration there is always at root a desire for mastery and manipulation. All the ego can do is to prepare itself for the coming-into-being of something which cannot be manipulated.

Intellectually I knew these things ad nauseam, but a ridiculous and crude drawing had sent me reeling. I felt myself lapping up against the shores of an inner ocean of excitement. It was, I kept repeating to myself, just too bizarre. I wanted to tell someone about it, but who could understand? Even Derek, with all his knowledge of Elizabethan alchemy, could not tell me that much. The serpent has to devour itself to release the Philosopher's Stone, the Lapis. In its embrace is the Golden Flower, the three jewels of the Abhidharma.

I rushed home forgetting everything else, but the experiment which I would perform in my own mental laboratory. I knew that I had found the secret of the projection mechanism and that it had found me.

5

The Light of Darkness[1]

In the darkness of the night you may open up a dialogue with yourself and arrive at a profound inner penetration. This does not consist in the free association of one's thoughts, but rather in their cessation; in the recognition that one possesses other voices within one. To a Jesuit or to an orthodox Catholic this might take the form of an open and naive dialogue with the Divine, but there is nothing which can disturb the utter silence of the effort and concentration involved in the meditation. The only disturbances come as lapses, as a recalling of consciousness to the point of discursive thinking. You are afraid to go further into the realm of unbeing, into the unravelling of being. Pushed to its extreme of unthinking, unconscious awareness it would take the form of an ascent into pure experience into the abeyance of the nagging thoughts which plague you and chain you to affects and emotions. There are gateways which come upon one in moments of crisis. Gateways which open up the paths towards illumination. To points at which hallucinations cease and are no longer sought.

How many times must you enter? These occasions bring

---

[1] This forms the fourth chapter of *The Quest for Gold*. It existed only in manuscript form in one of his diaries. No further chapters to the novel have been uncovered.

upon an inner circulation within the mental retort. Each stimulus calls forth responses which must be assimilated, but the essential nature of the stimulus remains the same. Rooted in an avatar, an archaic sense of the other being, you recoil in apprehension wondering whether or not this unfolding principle is hostile to life itself, wondering whether or not you have caught the tail of the Devil rather than the Divine Light.

It must happen countless times and with each experience it must happen on a different level so that gradually your prejudices and anticipations are inexorably eroded and so that you reach the point where the foundations of your being are so undermined that there is nothing to separate you from the free fall into it, other than the last saving glimmer of common sense.

Back in my flat I began to take out some of the papers, books, documents and paintings which had occupied me in the past three years. Many of them were now in packing cases and boxes ready for my move to another home. They represented to me my storehouse of hopes and treasures and a burden which had prevented me from leading a normal life. For their sake I had brought upon myself overwork, illness and debt and my relief came from a sense of a lifting of the burden, because for the first time my identity was no longer linked to them. A certain emancipation was taking place.

All throughout my self-imposed exile and near poverty as an artist I had withdrawn into my work for reasons which very few people could understand. Paintings are material objects and very often even the most abstract and intellectual exercises contained within them retain the clearest link with material and physical objective reality, for they deal in the raw stuff of the world, in images, colour, form and line and materials which are worked upon to produce a tangible product. But there is another kind of work which I have taken as my orientating point: the use of the materials for an exploration of the spiritual and metaphysical realm. In this way the materials become the medium by which the other realities and dimensions are manifested. Whether or not one has a conscious awareness of this is not ultimately relevant, for in the manifestation those realities or realms which are not directly connected with consciousness come forward with an immediacy which can strike one as revelatory. It's the discontinuity with one's everyday life which creates the impact of the revelation, for in manifesting itself the spiritual insight is a self-manifest. It comes of its own accord through a receptive medium. I was using my work, therefore, as a means of approaching an intuitive awareness without risking my own consciousness as the intermediary. Now, however, I was becoming increasingly prepared to take the risk and no longer use my work as the substitute for a transformation of my own consciousness. That is what I had found, the gateway within myself as an objective reality which could be approached equally in a spirit of objectivity rather than in one of crisis or desperation.

I had once received an early lesson in this approach to the opus with a minor catastrophe which had befallen some of my mystical landscapes. I had not looked at them for some time, and took them out one evening when I was feeling depressed and disappointed in order to encourage myself. One thing which distinguished them was their luminosity of colour, which created an atmosphere of impossible otherworldliness about them. They contained colours which are not contained in nature. Feeling already somewhat knocked about I was horrified to find that they had faded. I was looking at the same paintings, but somehow the spiritual light which they had contained had been extinguished. They had now become utterly dead to me; irrevocably lost. Ironically it is since this date that they have proved to be the most popular with my patrons who would rather buy a dead painting than a living one.

This event left me simply stunned. It struck a paranoid chord which must occur from time to time to any artist, for what is the artist without his work? So I sat and meditated and concluded that without my work I did not amount to very much. It had become a total obsession which had distorted my personality and which was making me incapable of relating in any other way. But I had tried and worked so hard upon it and upon myself and knew that I was sincere in what I was trying to do even if I could not control the results, or even if I had become prone at times to the neuroses which accompany an insecure lifestyle; paranoia being the chief of them. What else could I do? Did I care so little about my life that I was prepared to give it entirely to my work? For there were friendships and relationships which had broken under the burden of the work, to which I could not give at the critical crucial juncture, when one word spoken softly, but firmly, heals.

I sat alone in the silence of my living room on the third floor, up two narrow flights of stairs, in a shabby garret where the front door bell did not work and the plumbing did not work and where friends gradually did not visit as I stopped serving my celebrated Bohemian dinners. One of them had brought upon himself my ire for remarking that he would not have expected me to live in a place like that. He had expected a smart designer flat lined with book shelves and expensively framed paintings. Paradoxically he sat in the same chair that one of the Kuwaiti Princes had sat in with tears in his eyes, simply because no one else in London had invited him to their home. I was not ashamed of it, but I had become isolated and lonely in it, like thousands of others struggling upon the margins. In that environment you know that you can drop dead in the night and no one will be at all concerned or there at the final moment. Indeed the last occupant of my bedroom had gone in exactly that fashion and had remained seated in his armchair watching television for two weeks before we had found his rotting carcass. To his memory, and neglected life, I turned that room into an art gallery after one night when his spirit returned to knock the grate and produce banging noises in the walls where there were no pipes or loose fittings to rattle. In that room I had strange experiences and felt a presence which was not benign in its relationship to me. I would often tell it to get out or have the courage to show itself, daring it to materialise before me.

Experiences like that are of doubtful validity and objectivity, for the psychic nerve ending which is struck is invariably one's own, and the phenomena come as projections from one's psyche, even though one might not be able to regard the psyche as a personal possession. The episode with the paintings provoked that sort of response in me. It knocked me out of frame into a twilight state of consciousness.

Deep down we all know that it is an elaborate game, the meaning of which is unknown to us. In our worst moments we know that it is an exercise in futility and that our time which is so precious to us is nothing in the vastness of the cosmos. If that realisation truly comes to us we cannot be other than shaken to the core. What apparatus can you take along with you to measure infinity and its paradoxes? Can a human consciousness preoccupied with bank statements and love affairs that go wrong cope with the boundless infinitude? Yet artists go on creating and pouring their contents into the human vacuum as a solitary statement against the brutality of an unredeemed and corrupt material existence. I decided there and then that it did not matter to me and that I would go on and create objects of beauty in the full face of that realisation, to hold in balance if I could the opposing forces of creation and destruction.

I lay down with these thoughts and stared at the walls. A peculiar red light filtered through the wooden blinds and bounced off the corner of the room opposite me and splintered into a diffuse glowing vapour. The shadows of the furniture which I had collected in moments of bourgeois fancy stood out possessively. The whole room had become animated as if it were the objects in it which possessed me. I could just make out the gathering of the light and the materialisation of figures contained within it. There was a procession of a carnival like nature. Men and women dressed in robes were dancing around the solemn bearers of a litter upon which was seated a portly middle-aged man who was smiling at his followers. A young boy walked apace with the litter carrying a huge parasol fashioned in the shape of a lotus flower, and this protected the saintly one from the brilliant sunlight as he progressed towards the entrance of a temple. The litter was put down and he stepped from it and blessed the assembly who then vanished. Soon no more than his head and shoulders were left incongruously attached to my living room wall giving me a stern and reprimanding look.

"You arrogant young fool! You think you can hold it? You think that in your ignorance you can take on so much? Then try it and see if you are so strong as to look at the opposition."

I was now on my own listening to the silence rushing in upon the room. The vision had disappeared. I had pulled out my divan and taking out a spare quilt bedded down in the living room which had served originally as my bedsit before my expansion into the dead man's room. The shadow cast by the back of the divan loomed ahead of me and I felt curiously detached from the divan's support although my head was resting upon it. The room was extremely cold, and I lay there shivering. And then as I was about to dismiss the vision as yet another hallucination the light began to dart about the room, jumping from one plane to the next and gathering pace in a swirling, rhythmic movement. The spectrum of colours which the alchemists call the peacock's tail blazed past me like comets from the heavens. My inner eye registered colours never seen in the light of the daytime sun. Minuscule fragments of incredibly detailed views splintered before me, sharp, clear and defined as if illuminated in a laser light. There were mineral samples, plant forms and the progress of animals from the time of creation, all of them flashing past me in no more than an instant given to each holographic frame. Out of the ether was coalescing the face of a woman of fabulous beauty, a goddess with luxurious rings of auburn hair.

I felt I had rediscovered the magic kaleidoscope of my childhood. I used to sit transfixed for hours turning its chamber, watching the multicoloured patterns unfolding and with it reliving my nighttime adventures. I was no more than three or four when I broke open the chamber and pulled out the tinsel fragments which had so entertained me and thus broke also their spell upon me. I remembered that and recalled the dismembering of visions which comes with reductive analysis. But what did the Buddha mean by mentioning the opposition? I did not have to wait long for an answer.

Everything you see here is an illusion. This beautiful woman is nothing but a devil and she will use these visions to clothe herself and hide her true nature so that you will become fascinated by the illusion and ensnared in the black arts. You will think that you have created it and if that happens you will try to gain power through these mere conjurings. See them for what they are.

If there is such a thing as the spirit of ugliness, then I saw it. The devils which I had read about in the Buddhist literature as belonging to the night of initiation flocked about. People have been known to drop dead of fright and for a few moments I was scared, but I remembered that they were products of my imagination and after all possessed of no more reality than I would admit to and gave them full rein over the space around me. There was even a touch of comedy, because I recalled the scene in the film Raiders of the Lost Ark when the Ark of the Covenant is opened and instead of the dialogue with God there ensues the torment of demons. Eventually they left me and the room returned to its prosaic normality.

I got up and opened the window. Outside it was blowing up into a storm. The commotion of the wind shaking the trees in the back gardens and the clashing noise of a dustbin lid rolling on some concrete paving brought back to me my sense of hearing which for the past hour had deserted me. That was the weirdest part, I thought, for why would I suddenly go deaf when there was a frantic storm raging outside?

I returned to my bed and sat up continuing to gaze out of the window at the large London plane tree in the garden. The night was not yet over, for perched in the tree was the seated form of the Buddha.

"What am I to do about it?" I thought aloud.

He said it was very simple and that all I had to do was to give everything up and follow him. I can still hear his laughter and that was 21 months ago.

I did not forget that message and other similar messages came to me from that inner source, but their import I had to place on ice – suspending it temporarily as I plunged back into a very materialistic lifestyle. But even that had its twist, for I had never asked to become a business executive. It just happened and it threw me into a merry-go-round of committees and deadlines and gilded banquets which took me completely out of everything that had previously been my life. I gave up being an artist.

Selected diary entries for the period during the composition of *The Quest for Gold*

16.1.82

I also want to write, but more fundamentally I have to look at my spiritual life, and see what that means. I progress to peaks of awareness and insight and then fall back into the conditioned world and begin the cycle all over again. But what can one say in the face of my experiences? If the Buddha appears to you and shows you the way, as has happened to me on two occasions, how can you continue unchanged by it?

I have come closer to understanding what this means. For me retreating into the monastic life is out of the question. I believe in living in the world too much for that. No, it is a question of one's conscious development. Moving from occasional flashes of enlightenment to experiencing it in a sustained way. That really is the question and when it comes I must not shirk it, but accept it.

13.2.82

At the beginning of this particular period I had a dream which coincides with what John said about not trying too hard. The dream was far too long and detailed to summarise accurately at this stage, but the meaning was very clear indeed. It dealt with attaining Buddhahood and enlightenment. The dream itself was heavily hallucinogenic. It was spectacular and beautiful. At the culmination of it, the domed towers of the cathedral in Munich, burst into petals of flowers, and then suddenly contracted. As if a film was reversed and the action went backwards. The towers shrank into budlike forms, and then my own Buddha, myself in Buddha form spoke. He spoke of the No-path. Attaining Buddhahood, he said, was only possible when attaining Buddhahood was put to an end. The blossoming was curtailed and stopped, and with it the dream ended.

26.6.82

The last few weeks have witnessed very much a coming apart for me. Robin, the flat, Edinburgh, Davidh and the fact that I can't concentrate on my work. It's been so inexorable that it's very much like a re-run of events with Hedvig. I am convinced that she was practising black magic against me then, and it could also be the case now. My father is the only link these things have in common. He could well have relayed all these happenings in my life to her, and if she really is a dark spirit, as I think she is, it would be galling to her to think that she is missing out on these successes.

Davidh was the last link in the chain. I used him in the magic I had enacted to break the bond with her. It was my love for him that made me realise that it was crazy to continue with her.

Similarly it has been the awful way things went between us last week that made me make this connection.

Right now, however, I have been useless.

Anyway if she has put a voodoo onto me I have turned it back on her.

I am taking a long time to get my head together. I am in a state to be honest. Emotionally and physically. On Saturday after the Gay Pride March I couldn't stop thinking about Davidh. Last Tuesday's scene between us really hurt me. After all I thought all that was over between us, but that night I felt really depressed; tired, ill and vulnerable. I wanted to ignore him but he wouldn't let me, and then paid me back in full measure. Now that I've written to him it's all worse than ever. He will be full of indignation, hurt and outrage, and I want it all to be better and end well, but it's too late. It is highly unlikely that he will react sensibly and see how hurt I am through all those incriminating words .... It will either be a major scene or resentful stares and silences.

17.7.82

The usual Saturday exhaustion. The Edinburgh scheme has reached the finishing straight and it remains for me to do the sectional perspective and interior proposals. 5 sheets of drawings are now out of the way and another 7 can now easily be finished. Therefore this weekend and over the next three days after that I still have much to do.

I've now had Davidh's "reply". One of S------'s administration people have written back saying that there is no Davidh W------- there. Now I know that Davidh has received and read that letter. His reaction would not make any sense if he had not read it. At the same time it is clear to me that it has been thoroughly read and gone over. Comments in various hands have been scrawled over the envelope, and the letter itself looks somewhat worn. It didn't have to be opened if he wasn't there or if I got the name wrong because the envelope had an address on it.

It makes me sad that he should resort to this kind of tacky Catch 22 situation. If it is genuine, then it doesn't say much either for the people at S------. It has taken 3 weeks for them to send it back. Well., ...

Davidh rejects direct communication and dialogue. That has always been the problem, and this response is only the latest illustration of that. If he is behind it, it shows how dishonest he can be. My only response can be to be direct and call his bluff.

I had an enjoyable evening with father, Peter and Liz. But went on to Heaven where I had a less scintillating time.

This thing with Davidh reveals a perennial problem with me. Whenever I make an occasional demand on people to rise above a situation or to respond they fail. It has now happened COUNTLESS times.

I've had another thought about this letter business. Since it was posted on Friday it occurs after the peculiar evening in Subway. Davidh was sizing me up and watching me in action with other people, and this is his way of saying, no you're no different with other people. He has made a judgement and he intends to stick by it. It is yet another one of his insults.

Re-reading my letter I am not ashamed of it. It is actually quite calm in tone, and bearing in mind how strongly I felt it is pretty low key, although it remains highly critical.

I don't know why John[1] should so much want to hurt me and lash out the way he does. He is the one who has been trying to change me into things that I am not.

---

[1] He has written "John" in the diary, but "Davidh" is intended.

Thursday night saw some strange experiences. I engaged in a very long meditation and went further than I have ever gone. The way in which it came on spontaneously after a long period of concentration on things of this world took me by surprise. It seems the way is open for me at any time.

I had also a strange communication with Davidh. This came into my thoughts also very spontaneously and was again very surprising. It burst through as a question and it must have been at about 2.00 a.m., [when] John[2] would have been out clubbing and mulling over the way my letter was returned, and he came up with this question: "Why? Why are you destroying yourself?"

It was at this point that I broke off my meditation and told him in a long dialogue, or rather monologue, that I want to die and don't want another earthly incarnation. I told him however, that I do indeed love him very much and would want to share my life with him and said we should stop all these games immediately and that perhaps on Friday we could make a start. His reply was that it was too soon, and I can now see why. He did add though, "Why can't we just be a couple?"

What struck me as genuine about this telepathy trip was that it contained expressions and questions that are not part of my vocabulary and mentation.

This impressive bout of meditation contained some beautiful hallucinations. I materialised the tree of life and the serpens to demonstrate the power of the psyche to Davidh and Elaine!

---

[2] "John" written instead of "Davidh".

18.7.82

If I can get Peter to work with me next week I can have Edinburgh under my belt. From now on the decks have to be cleared and the low key day-and-a-half I've had forgotten. I am depressed and worried about a hundred and one things, but the show must go on. Davidh's way of reply to me is despicable. He felt my writing to him via S--- was a further intrusion into his Territory, and he replied with an intrusion into mine. Giving my intimate and private letter to someone else to reply to is not only an act of cowardice, but also tramples upon my integrity and privacy. My right to have feelings of my own. After all Davidh is a private affair for me. I haven't talked about it, and so it's my own pain. It's a horrible situation we've got into, and he shows no ability or willingness to get out of it. All he can do is escape and God knows what from, because he is not escaping from me; only himself.

Somewhat against better judgement I went on to Subway, being unable to get into these drawings. I had the feeling John[3] would be there, but not seeing him I had just reconciled myself to being without him when suddenly he popped up. The atmosphere between us is now unbearably heavy, and it is becoming quite ugly. I can't say it is entirely coming from me because I don't feel any ill-will towards him, but it is clear that he's pretty ill-disposed towards me. He is even following me about from space to space, and I vice-versa. We collide in the loo, the back bar, the upstairs bar, ad nauseam. I had just about had enough when they started showing the movie "Shivers".

The professor remarks, "The virus is like a combination

---

[3] "John" written instead of "Davidh".

between venereal disease and an aphrodisiac. The person who created it thought we're animals who think too much, and he wanted to see a return to instinct."

Well, quite appropriate, I thought. The sort of bad taste synchronicity indulges in. (I had just started having a discharge.) In a grizzly way I felt like saying to John,[4] "This seems to be like your kind of movie." Having got thoroughly sick of it, John beat me to the door, and soon after I left also. For some reason I felt compelled to go to where I know he parks the VW. It wasn't there, but as I walked down headlights came round the corner, and there he was driving past me.

It was too much. I felt physically sick and kicked a few parking meters in anger. A display of desperation which he would have seen in his rear-view if he was of a mind to look back.

It's become something of a psychic duel, and heaven knows what he is thinking because it must be freaking him out as well.

19.7.82

I am shattered. A VERY tough day. Uphill on the work and unsatisfactory progress.

Tomorrow is the day I have to finalise the interior proposal and push the plans out.

I have introduced Peter to the work scene and with luck he will do a good job of the sectional perspective for me.

With Davidh I now finally capitulate. I give in. It is not worth pursuing now and if not now, then never. He has

---

[4] "John" written instead of "Davidh".

managed to have the last word and I will let him have it, because to try to enter into any further dialogue would be useless. It would constantly come back to me, and the scenes would get progressively more violent. It is also part of a trend. This year has been one of unprecedented emotional friction and disappointment. I have very few contacts or relationships intact and have not committed myself to any new ones. It's been one long drawn out emotional bloodbath with no success on my part in either winning through to any understanding or reconciliation, let alone, change. Everyone around me seems hell bent on their grim track, whereas I seem to be even more than ever the slave of my ideas and projects. I can't break out of it and it seems my efforts to reach other people are doomed and futile.

But more than ever I have tried to do what I feel is right. I have tried to follow through difficult and often painful decisions, with honesty and moral truth as my guides. I may be deluded and I may have become aggressive, intolerant, demagogic and demanding, but I haven't been master in my house, master of my fate.

It has been painful all along. I feel that in all my most recent relationships I have been led along and then dropped in the shit, with the consequences within my own hands and with others ducking their responsibility in common and shared situations. It is a thread which runs through all these sagas. The feeling of a lack of reciprocity, of give and take.

To lose two friends in the space of a week is perhaps the result of negligence on my part, but then I don't think Davidh or Robin really were friends, and I only made them so in fantasy or out of need. Something at each time with which to fill the emotional vacuum; the absence of love.

But with John[5] psyching me out I cannot go to these dives and discos any more. I don't want his psychological games, because that is what it amounts to. I mustn't forget that he is a primitive in his unconscious. I put the evil eye on you. But underneath he's like that - like so many people barely conscious of his malevolence.

My view of the world is becoming increasingly paranoiac. Black magic, psychic powers, influences. But I think they are objectively real quantities.

How can I expect his thanks for saying in effect that his life is a sham and he must change? Too many people wish me ill, I know that.

Today was tough. Grueling. But I have four more days like it ahead of me. Days in which I have to be in control.

I will seek solace and advice from the I Ching ...

NOW for DAVIDH

Hsü/Waiting (Nourishment)
"The rain will come in its own time. We cannot make it come; we have to wait for it."
"One is faced with a danger that has to be overcome. Weakness and impatience can do nothing."
"We should not worry and seek to shape the future by interfering in things before the time is ripe."
9 AT THE BEGINNING:
"The danger is not yet close ... there is a feeling of something impending. One must continue to lead as regular life as possible ... "

---

[5] "John" written instead of "Davidh".

6 AT THE FOURTH:
"Waiting in blood.
Get out of the pit."
"The situation is extremely dangerous. It is of utmost gravity now - a matter of life and death. Bloodshed seems imminent. There is no going forward or backward; we are cut off as if in a pit. Now we must simply stand fast and let fate take its course. This composure, which keeps us from aggravating the trouble by anything we might do, is the only way of getting out of the dangerous pit."

That certainly gives a lot to think about.

Six at the top is a good summary of what happened with Hedvig.

No wonder I feel paranoid.

In my earlier comments I think I judged things right, alas. It's almost a situation in which I could expect the fucker to try to kill me. I could even trigger off a psychotic breakdown in him.

Although I asked this about Davidh, I actually think it applies to my health. Davidh is the immediate paranoid and fantastic reaction.

It wouldn't be the first time the I Ching has answered the wrong question.

I think I am on the terminal trip. What I need is first rate counselling on how to deal with the consequences of serious illness and going through operations. If I can't face it, I know I will die.

I am on the point of total physical collapse.

In a cheerful mood though!

20.7.82

That was a heavy night all right. These I Ching trips can cut close to the bone. Very much of a confrontational night. Confrontation with the psyche. Having this come up in connection with Davidh, whether it applies to him or not does coincide with a fear I have with the ways things went. It is rather a re-run of Omar, Hedvig, Terence. However, it would be prudent not to provoke any further encounters. At least not for the time-being. Nonetheless, these things cannot be avoided if they happen synchronistically.

I was so freaked that I almost expected Davidh to turn up on my doorstep, wielding an axe. I went out for air and saw a red VW van parked outside. It was almost like something out of a film. I walked towards it slowly and carefully expecting Davidh to leap out.

*

Today has been more productive and constructive. My interior scheme takes shape. Peter is beginning to progress with the perspective, and from now I have only one more presentation drawing to push out.

A pleasant bonus. Another letter from Robin. It's good to see that things are going much better for him.

31.7.82

Edinburgh has finally come to rest, but at quite a cost. The presentation was well concluded, but at the expense of two all-night sessions, which surprisingly did not completely do me in. I was immensely satisfied to get to the end of it in spite of the constant uphill struggle all around.

3.8.82

The debacles continue. Monday was spent rushing around on the finishing touches to the Edinburgh Report and presentation. It all resolved itself after the hassles of Friday, with reasonable points and an all-round effort from me and Ted.

I stayed over Monday night with Ted and Mary and went up to Edinburgh with Martyn today.

The whole scheme has fallen down on Plot Ratio. It has to come down from the present 3.63 to 2.8 at least. An elementary thing has totally screwed up the overall effort, and we begin all over again.

Edinburgh was beautiful in this sweltering heat.

24.8.82

It's a real handicap to be feeling this ill because I'm paralysed today. Another day in bed. I must really grapple now with the most essential tasks and prepare to move.

I have to galvanize myself into action and forget about all residual disappointments. I have to forget about my isolation and lost friendships and the indifference and inabilities of my family. I even have to forget that I am ill at present. If I cannot forget these things I might as well commit suicide ....

A very peculiar incident. Earlier I'd missed Davidh at Subway since I was not dressed according to the code. This was after an enjoyable visit to Hampstead and a depressing visit to Bangs which left me feeling suicidal.

No sooner had I got home than I determined to go back and have it out with him. I jumped into a cab in the same mood of inspired resolution which led to my leaving C------ [Auditors]. At Westminster Bridge I pulled the cab up because I thought I saw my father leaning on a parapet.

This false connection led to my missing Davidh.

I am pretty amazed by what has happened. We were literally kept apart.

13.9.82

Incredibly congested weeks with my time spent more and more in ------. Many things have become more resolved and in some ways this has been the most enjoyable part of the year. Edinburgh is in for planning and barring disasters at my next planning meeting, the work should be at an end. L------- T ------- Square is virtually there, as far as the funding document goes. It is just about on the point of printing.

My personal life is more settled at the moment with James S------ in my life – barring a hiccup at the first hurdle of a visit to the clinic.

Strange experience with Ariel who is having a full blown breakdown. I'll write about that in full later.

I am EXHAUSTED, however.

I can almost look back on an enormously satisfying achievement over the year. But today was revolting, jumping up and running over the place.

14.9.82

I've started writing again. Beginning with Ariel. This thing could well write itself. I am determined to be disciplined about it and write 10 pages daily. I'm not making a work of art out of it. It's for money and for my goal of going all the way. Since it's closely tied into insanity as a principle theme, even with the first day I've had some uncomfortable moments.

18.9.82

One sour moment this week occurred with Davidh, another one of our encounters. The psychic side is still all there and with all the intensity that involves. He is still phenomenally resentful and unapproachable. It's one of those situations where you can do absolutely nothing.

*

Another encounter with him tonight. I attached a letter to his van. Brief - unemotional, unlike the one I posted and the others which never got posted. I think that now it will be settled. We will either have an almighty row or become proper friends. But either way it is now in the open.

If it is resolved I will have had to fight fantastically hard for Davidh. I have never been so far to the brink with anyone else. I laid myself on the line and was stabbed in the psyche for it. In many ways I don't know how I stood up to it because he has directed so much energy against me.

Now, however, he cannot run away and I won't let him. In the meantime Edinburgh depresses me.

23.10.82

Vasilis: Ariel will be all right. It will take a few weeks or months, but he will be all right. Go and see him. You might learn something from him, even if you won't get to that level. But Ariel still needs help. He's got many problems.

Andrew: Now look here, don't give me that shit. I know what Ariel's problems are. I've spent time with him and that's why I cannot help. You can't do it either. No one can. Only Ariel can do it himself, and I know because I've been there many times. Listen, no one can do it for him. They can only pretend. It's the same with the psycho-therapists - they only think they make people recover. They're just projecting their own power complexes. You have to feel it here.

As usual I get more upset thinking about it. It just won't do. The same old problem.

3.11.82

60. Che/Limitation
"Not going out of the gate brings misfortune."

27.11.82

Chapter 3 - Brief Synopsis Note.
Must be concerned with the LAPIS

It can go in several directions - It can talk about my experience of painting or it can attempt the arduous course of completely new directions. Arduous because they demand to be lived first of all. My present urgent circumstances won't permit that. It is clear that in the last few weeks I have come close to having a breakdown, and going further down that road won't get me anywhere at all. No one will look after me if I am ill. At the same time, I am not Ariel. Definitely not. I'm a tougher, sharper character and have to be true to form, I have to come out of this as a 9 to 5 person to maintain my sanity and to give me enough time to get through to the next stage. I will get on to it. This is THE terminal trip. The ONLY worthwhile goal in the universe, but it mustn't be terminal too soon. As the alchemists say, "Not a few died in pursuit of the goal" - to paraphrase.

2.12.82

A calmer week which makes the experience of the last few weeks appear more like a case of projection. I must really have been close to cracking up altogether and am thankful that I seem to have pulled through quickly. If I hadn't seen Ted last Sunday I would have gone over the edge most certainly. As it is I almost feel as though nothing has happened, with the exception that I am feeling quite ill. In fact I don't know, but even though I am not on the brink mentally I am on the brink physically. The disturbance has simply shifted its emphasis. So the crisis still continues. However, I am grateful to both Ted and my father for their supportive attitude.

Last night was a busy one in the dreams it produced. A very long dream in which I was running away from a group of two women and a man who were out to give me a beating. I realised the futility of running away and faced them. The man attacked me and I fell to the ground and felt the force of the blow. A wound appeared at the side of my head where my glasses had smashed against it. I got up and wrestled with the figure, brought him to the ground and won the fight with him. After that we had sex and became lovers as the two black women looked on approvingly.

The images were terribly familiar and were from dreams I have had on many occasions.

It certainly was a BIG dream.

There is also an obvious parallel with Davidh. So we just wait to see how all this will go for me. But I am determined to pursue it right through. Robin, Davidh and Elaine are going through similar experiences. Interesting enough R and E are reacting the same way to Ted. Our "union" and association is no accident. I feel VERY strongly that they are my psychical family.

Thinking about the dream, I cannot help wondering whether there will be a correspondence to it.

The events of last Saturday will when they sink in drive Davidh bananas. I was projecting back at him what he projected onto me and my voyeurism of his "performance" in the fuck room even struck me as being odd. I really had a very strong desire to kick him in the behind whilst he was sucking another guy off. The last episode was sparked off by a less extreme reaction on my part. I feel the logical outcome of Davidh's whole attitude is violence and I cannot help thinking that sooner or later it will come to that.

As for me, I now feel VERY ill. It reminds me of the time just before our final rift when I was in Edinburgh I dreamt that I was seriously ill and I was being carried off on a stretcher to Intensive Care. Someone remarked, "He really is done for," and a group of people were waiting for news anxiously. Immediately after that Davidh and I bust up over his remark, "I don't want to catch your disease," and I was very ill at the time; hence the vehemence of my reaction.

4.12.82

I've been very close to the depths in the past few days.

What really stimulated this crisis was the Canterbury carving. The vision on its own was complete. It required no analysis because it was so clear. The Canterbury carving however is an iconographic work which has amalgamated to it so many aspects of the symbols. In my vision I feel they were unambiguous and fully experienced and understood. At Canterbury what I got was a dose of cultural confusion. This struck to the roots of Christianity and has underlined for me once more what a pernicious doctrine and creed it is. I have no doubt that the historical Christ was a Buddha, but the historical church became a force for evil and was turned over to the Devil very early on in its history.

I have the feeling that practically nothing was left of the original teaching of Christ and that the whole cultural milieu of the Christian epoch is an abysmal mish mash of the Roman mystery religions, Alchemy and Gnosis and the other deeper Pagan elements. Reading about Alchemy I am not surprised that the alchemists did not reach their goal. They could not, because they saw everything from a Christian standpoint. Their experiment was contaminated from the start by the powerful symbolism of Christianity - and it is so powerful because it corresponds with the personal consciousness of its practitioners.

11.12.82

Continuing to be very depressed indeed. Manic mood swings. But then I have reason to be depressed. Depression is not an accident and illness. It is a psychic reaction, albeit violent, an attempt to restore equilibrium. At the same time I have been aware of the root causes and have been unable to act on them. That's the crux. It's a response to a sense of inner violation; the transgression of natural law.

The symbols at Canterbury really did disturb me because they contain so much which is paradoxical and contradictory to the conventional notion of church. My initial feeling was that they connoted the Devil; that they were tantamount to giving over the church to the Devil. A secret sign which undermined the whole work. Or else, through the Alchemical allusions, you could say that the secret is so secret that one would never suspect how secret it is. That is the essence of a secret. So inexplicable is it that you would not suspect, unless already initiated, that the Devil and Christ are one. There is not the slightest doubt about this interpretation, which seemed perfectly right and fitted the symbols, and the fundamental nature of symbolism itself. Now that is a real mystery.

12.12.82

The sharpness and suddenness of this mood swing surprises me. I am going through a roller coaster. Friday night, suicidal depression - Saturday again the same - Sunday: stabilising/enjoyment. Three days of good sex, on the town spending money. Today feeling really fine; calm, contented, resigned - then WHAM into the pits again. The disturbance is ricocheting through my psyche. It is triggering off centre after centre. It appears to me working through everything. The worst thing is that all vestiges of a normal structure have completely broken down. I am unable to function, to put it bluntly.

Where does all this lead to? I'm perfectly sane, know what's going on, know that I am progressing all the time and that this is a necessary period of crisis. It's an attempt to find a new centre at the point of being on the edge - but it's really close.

17.12.82

Downswing - Walking to E----- the other morning I pulled a tendon and am now in agony. The cold of the last few days has given me a swollen face. I only noticed what a state I was in late last night in Subway. Not wishing to go home I drank my way out of depression - an uncharacteristic move - or rather to forestall it.

Today I am totally exhausted.

4 hours in the club vanished. John and I simply talked like lunatics and probably sounded like lunatics. The best conversation. Fruits of the Neumann - a replacement copy now bought.

I'm still not out of the woods. The disturbance is recirculating like a spiral. It continues to move to new centres.

Last night's dream:-

The divine child was ill with a form of brain cancer. I watched an operation on his skull with the exposed tissue. To my surprise when it was completed there were no signs of scars. The surgeon said the operation was a success but only a partial one – the beneficial result would last a year and a half and the effect would wear off.

Many dreams recently. Active interface.

I haven't dug myself out of the pit yet. Facing it, holding it, equalising it.

However everything fits into a pattern now. I am without a role these days and I am also being sat upon creatively. I wouldn't mind, but at the same time, I have no direction given to me. I am forced out on my own and am on my own without the benefits of independence.

I know I am in a deep crisis. Everything is coming to a head by virtue of the fact that this year has seen no fundamental change in my life - only an intensification of everything that has gone before.

But it is really curious. I have become totally isolated. The only friends I now have are people in the same position.

I really don't know what the way out is. If I knew I would take it. I certainly did not chose this course. I am simply here.

2.1.83

Shifting sands. I have to move, and I'll repeat history and move to my father's, but it could be a disaster, given the deterioration in things with T-------. I hope now that I have gone right down and have tapped the hidden well that I can pump up the treasure and forge into 1983 as a hero.

Punishment for the Transgressors

Actaeon and Marsyas pose the question
Of why gods so savagely guard their domains
From wanton and unwanted transgressions
Where no laurels crown the victor
Where trespassers fall to silent martyrdom
See Marsyas torn from his skin
By calculating Apollo
Actaeon pulled down by Artemis' driven hounds
His stag's head pointing to the psychological
For this is no youthful artist's vision
Not by accident did ancient Titian wield his brush
Clear sighted and unblurred
By gods, madonnas, satyrs and martyrs
Tuned to his most sombre meditation
Sated by colours and flesh enough to feast voluptuaries
Turned to nature seen by candlelight
To its flickering wavering silence
To the raging emptiness of its storms
Thus Holy places are approached
Out of time
Not through acts of pilgrimage,
Yearnings for deliverance and sacrifices
They are slipped into sideways
By stealth, concentration and accident
Fallen into when we are exhausted
When we encounter the eternal moment

Where laughing, crying and confused
We catch hold of the unholdable
And fall out again.

Then how grey the world appears in vain swept November
After we dutifully took our dose of culture
Lingering as students or tourists over paintings
Of doe-eyed virgins and scarcely digested mythologies
Which touch us not
When our city madness passes for sanity
In its restlessness and acts of acquisition
This is the Apollonian order
Against which Marsyas offended
Through freedom of spirit and absence of institution
Forming art from castoffs
And to Apollo we pay homage
After him turning butchery to an art
Playing the eternal game of stags and wolves
Passing over the holy grounds which haunt us still
Where Artemis and Apollo preside as the royal pair
So we recoil from these connections
From the closeness of creation to destruction
Unable to hold them together in one ground
As projections of man's mind
When it is the inner storm by which we a torn
As guardian of our own recesses and powers
Like adult primitives afraid of fire
Caught between madness and crucifixion
Always preferring the Pantheons
To freedom from gods

22.9.84

Finishing that book (by Kerényi)[1] has left my head whirling. Especially putting my thoughts down to Peter. The essential impression from the book is that the Greeks created their literature and art and architecture out of a direct communion with the gods which gave everything a meaning and a form. In that sense, in the direct line of contact, they too acquired god like abilities and genius.

I can sense that myself. Reading the Kerényi, the Greek gods come alive as real forces - one can feel their pulse and what it meant to experience Zeus. I am sure that following that feeling would lead similarly even now to great art and literature. Walking around the V & A I sensed it in the Donatello and Michelangelo casts. The great spirit of antiquity.

Consequently I've been undergoing another coniunctio experience and feel pretty shaken about. I don't know whether I can last it out and stay the course. And if I cannot whether others can follow. It is only by talking to other people that I am beginning to realise my experience is pretty unique.

The question is how to bring it to completion.

23.9.84

A terrible night's sleep leaves me feeling devastated. A 2.00 p.m. start to the day tells is own tale. I had a very vivid dream to which I returned in my thoughts several

---

[1] Carl Kerényi, *Zeus and Hera, Archetypal Image of Father, Husband and Wife.* Princeton University Press. 1975.

times between waking and sleeping.

The dream was about a Mafia family in which the same incests and dramas are enacted. As the wife lies dying of cancer the husband is knocking it off with the mistress with whom he has already moved in.

I remember being a bit shocked by the dream, which concludes with the "hero" (in this case the anti-hero) being bumped off by a Mafia hit squad. I suppose that's the corrective to too starry eyed a view of Greek mythology. But it occurs to me from Kerényi that the nucleus of the Greek religious experience is the celebration of the hieros gamos. Hence the double chambers at the temples at Paestum - The implication is of course that the highest forms of cultural expression come from the coniunctio attitude.

NATIONAL GALLERY

Room 20
SAMSON & DELILAH – RUBENS

Room 9
DEATH OF ACTAEON - TITIAN

Begun 1559, reworked 1570s - intended for Phillip II's collection. Shows Actaeon with a stag's head attacked by his hounds, but significantly it shows Diana in hot pursuit holding a bow as if firing with invisible strings and arrows. This makes it abundantly clear that the hounds are not Actaeon's thoughts as Bruno would have it, but Diana's Dactylloi. The painting shows Actaeon falling as if struck by Diana.

Room 29
JUDITH IN THE TENT OF HOLOFERNES - JOHANN LISS

The castration theme is a common one in art: c/f: Apollo flaying Marsyas - Also the wounding or killing of men by women/Diana and Actaeon/Judith and Holofernes/Samson and Delilah. These themes were especially beloved of the Neapolitan School after Caravaggio, and of course Artemisia is a prime proponent of the genre. The National Gallery unfortunately possesses none of her work, and this very rapid survey shows that the theme is thin on the ground, although looking at the Titian is very helpful and confirms my suspicion that Tom Moore's interpretation is quite off the track.

The history of art invariably links women to the theme of the castration of men and this points to the operation of a basic archetype contained within the Actaeon myth.

24.9.84

Going back to the beginning of Zeus and Hera. I am reminded by the Titian treatment of Diana and Actaeon that those who trespassed on the holy sanctuary at Likaion were thought to be transformed into wolves - or hunted deer. Therefore going back on this neither interpretation alone fits the facts of the myth - one must take both. The deer is an archetypal symbol of the hunted.

One aspect of the "transgression" motif which recurs throughout the literature is very worrying. Seeking after spiritual enlightenment is supposed to be very worthwhile and "worthy", but the gods also punish those who observe them with premature death or insanity. This is a paradox which is real enough and true enough, but it is not one which rewards virtue.

The other problem is what does one do with these insights and visions, but communicate them in the form of art? As yet there is no conceptual structure which can accommodate them. Similarly individuation must lead to something - but the experience of it appears to be a constant lurching forward. You hit a peak or surge of awareness, and equally you can be struck down and crippled in the intervening period of non-enlightenment. Obviously this is not very satisfactory either.

In all these respects I feel that I am doing all I can and have consistently been doing so, but I have not been the one in control of this fate - The only control I have had lies in the digging out of "lightening" realisation from the chaos. That was the quality I personally could bring to my experiences. Equally I could have been engulfed by darkness.

*

Dream 1. Last night I dreamt that John drew up my horoscope - A major crisis was pointed to in January, but the following months were "blissfully happy" ones. The dream had a mood of contentment and fulfilment about it.

Dream 2. In another dream I dreamt I had changed my surname and had chosen the name "Maier" - After the 17th century alchemist John Maier. It could well be my future nom de plume. "VOYAGE INTO NIGHT" is the title I have for some time settled upon for the poems.

Dream 3. A very brief fragment: I left a large cigar burning in an ashtray.

22.10.84[2]

Given my present mood I have decided to tackle the Actaeon theme directly. It contains perhaps THE central question and it is one which psychologically I can no longer leave aside, unchallenged and unanswered. It is the question of why it is that the Actaeons are turned into stags and punished for daring to look upon the gods. Or why the individuant who dutifully strives for self-realisation and enlightenment stumbles across the sorts of barriers which I keep on encountering: perverse destiny, negligent fates and castrating relationships.

The legitimate answer to me is not Shakespeare's line of where angels fear to tread or the martyrdom and self-denial of the saint but recognition and reward. Laurel leaves as opposed to thorns. But patently human history turns its back upon such a course.

The images I want to take are well known to me: the two paintings by Titian - the work of Artemesia Gentileschi and the inner encounter and experience of the Self.

Now I am quite clear in my mind also that if Hameed saw fit to present me with a cheque - totally unlikely as that would be - I would head straight for the hills. At the moment I really desperately need solitude. Solitude, peace and quiet and gentle countryside. Country lanes - autumn-leaves under foot. Real contact with nature. Good basic boots to walk in - a back pack and an anorak. Because at the moment I just see the city as a sick environment.

---

[2] *Punishment for the Transgressors* was composed on this day.

TITIAN'S paintings.

DIANA the huntress takes fire with a bow with invisible strings - All the action follows the movement of her right arm holding invisible strings and her outstretched left arm which holds the bow. Actaeon already transformed into a man with stag's head recoils along the direction of her aim as the hounds pin him down. Trees and foliage bend also in the same direction as if responding to the goddess' aim - clouds move rapidly - the light is flickering, as if to be extinguished - At the moment before a fierce storm. A stream rushes also in the same direction, towards Actaeon as he is about to be cut down. Actaeon is shown correctly with stag's head: body untransformed. The meaning of the transformation is psychological. The stag nature, woundedness and being pursued is in the head.

Observation of the landscape and still life of plants and climbing ivy is naturalistic. But his is the gloomy and funereal side of the vision.

A distant avenue of trees and what appears to be a horseman. The handling of the paint is highly impressionistic and from close-to forms are barely intelligible.

*

Reflecting on the wolf/stag emblem I am coming round to the view that this is a cultural problem - a problem of society as opposed to the individual: the fact that within our culture the cultivation of the spiritual life is almost impossible. Adaptation of the spiritual life is almost impossible. Adaptation appears to lie in its thorough repression and institutionalisation. Marsyas is a free spirit - He makes art with what he finds, and this freedom is what offends against the Apollonian order and is savagely butchered.

*

I cannot say that writing that poem has in any way put me in a better mood or led to a lightening. On the contrary it's made me feel really worn, and has given me a head-ache.

Psychologically though I feel it's on-the-line. Responsibility for the archetypes rests with us. We can't feel wounded or pursued by the collective unconscious when that is also a part of us. That is a statement of self-division which stands in the way of self-fusion as an almighty obstacle which must be hacked down. Studying the archetypes in mythology is another way in which we can stumble over ourselves. They come back to life as autonomous complexes, archetypes or beings and start to be charged up by the attention and libido we're giving them. This enhances their autonomy and tendency to take over and diminish the control of the Ego, with the danger that there is insufficient activity from the coordinating centre of the Self. The figure of Marsyas could almost stand as an image of the Self, unmoved by the tortuous goings on of all the Archetypes and complexes around it: somehow serving to hold them together, maintaining the tension.

Symbols of Creation and Destruction[1]

I

There is clearly a fine dividing line between inspiration and madness and this is something which Jung frequently refers to:-

> "Experiences of this kind are not without their dangers, for they are also ... the matrix of the psychoses." (CW9 Part I: *The Archetypes of the Collective Unconscious* - Page 351, Para 621.)

In view of this, the lack of concentration upon the connection between the alchemical literature and its symbolisms with the unconscious transformation symbolism found in the material of individual patients is a serious omission and is something of an embarrassment for an evaluation of Jung's work as a psychologist.

On the matter of the potential dangers involved in contact with the unconscious, we have sufficient hints in Jung's

---

[1] This chapter comprises extracts from an essay Andrew wrote as his "answer to Jung". It seems that in its original form this essay was given the title "The Antinomian Divide"; and was began circa 1980. The 1980 manuscript has been lost. Andrew prepared this version with the amended title in 1985 about six months before his death.

work as to encourage us to approach the subject with caution. We also know from his autobiographical memoir *Memories, Dreams and Reflections* that early on in his career he himself experienced episodes of near breakdown which bordered on psychosis. It was also during this period that he had an experience of the synchronistic and parapsychological phenomena which appear to accompany such episodes. Some insight into these matters can be provided by the luminous mandala drawings executed by him and by his visionary prose poem *Sermones ad Mortuos*. We find that when we encounter such experiences we are indeed not only in the grip of a fascination with the unconscious which can be so strong as to permit of such phenomena as automatic writing and "possession", but we also find ourselves faced with philosophical, existential and religious questions which can challenge us to the core of our being. This much can be sensed in Jung's *Sermones*:-

"Harken: I begin with nothingness. Nothingness is the same as fullness. In infinity full is no better than empty. Nothingness is both empty and full. As well might ye say anything else of nothingness, as for instance, white is it, or black, or again, it is not, or it is. A thing that is infinite and eternal hath no qualities, since it hath all qualities."

In view of what Jung has told us of the nature of the psychosis of modern man, with their tendency towards an unconscious expression of the will to power, it would be well for us to reflect upon these issues before we consider the meaning of his alchemical researches. In his essay *The Psychology of the Unconscious* he refers convincingly to the possibility of triggering off latent psychosis as a result of analytical work and, moreover, suggests that those who do so succumb to the negative effects of the unconscious can be the most apparently normal and adapted of us:-

> "... since the analytical technique activates the unconscious and brings it to the fore, in these cases the healthful compensation is destroyed, the unconscious breaks forth and in the form of uncontrollable fantasies and overwrought states which may, in certain circumstances, lead to mental disorder and possibly even to suicide. Unfortunately these latent psychoses are not so very uncommon." (CW7: *Two Essays on Analytical Psychology* - Page 112 Para 192)

Thus we find that in dealing with the unconscious and its manifestations we must cultivate a very broadminded approach, for we will come across experiences which will disorientate and confuse us and which at the same time exert upon us a compulsion in the experience of numinous images which appear to speak to us from "another realm". When we experience a glimpse into that other reality, the reality of the objective psyche, we are in the position of the spectator in *Burnt Norton* of seeing visions in the most commonplace of locations. It is then that our framework of reality can break down, and with it our seemingly secure foundations within the empirical, material world; all the more so if our concept of reality is too superficially normal and narrow to begin with. Nor do we need to look at the casualties of analysis for examples of such break-downs, for the same casualties arise out of our drug culture and these are not so very uncommon either. Indeed there are similarities between the hallucinatory experiences we have in taking LSD and those of an encounter with the objective psyche. Perhaps the only difference between the two is that of intensity, and the fact that the visionary experiences of active imagination may be the product of mental discipline and concentration and are not "trips" in the drug-induced sense. However, one should be cautious in even making such a distinction, because the drug-induced hallucinations can be so extraneous and overwhelmingly visual that there need be no danger of connecting with them.

A psychological crisis arises out of the irruption of contents from the unconscious which the conscious ego-attitude and personality finds contradictory and threatening. It also arises out of the difficulties involved in understanding and assimilating fantasy and dream material which refers to ideas at the borderline between a delusionary and an inspired state. Of this he says:-

"The reason why the involvement looks like a psychosis is that the patient is integrating the same fantasy material to which the insane patient falls victim, because he cannot integrate it but is swallowed up by it." (CW14: *Mysterium Coniunctionis* - Page 531 Para 756)

Jung's understanding of the psyche involves us in an uncomfortable recognition of the potential the unconscious has for activity which is inimicable to life itself; as if there is indeed an unconscious death wish. In this connection, Jung refers to the possibility that there are some individuals whose lives are fundamentally not viable and in whom there is not sufficient will to live. Such suggestions might strike us as being highly controversial, but on this and similar issues, Jung's comments are unequivocable:-

"If the demand for self-knowledge is willed by fate and is refused, this negative attitude may end in real death. The demand would not have come to this person had he still been able to strike out on some promising by-path. But he is caught in a blind alley from which only self-knowledge can extricate him ... Usually he is not conscious of his situation, either, and the more unconscious he is the more he is at the mercy of unforeseen dangers: he cannot get out of the way of a car quickly enough, in climbing a mountain he misses his foothold somewhere, out skiing he thinks he can negotiate a tricky slope, and in an illness he suddenly loses the courage to live. The unconscious has a thousand ways of snuffing out a meaningless existence with surprising swiftness." (CW14: *Mysterium Coniunctionis* - Page 472, Para 675.)

Thus if we accept Jung's model for the relations between the ego and the unconscious we find it is an enshrined oppostionalism where the unconscious has the potential to take an adversarial role. Moreover, it is a relationship which is of such a critical variety that if we slip up in our conscious attitude we can find ourselves at the mercy of uncontrollable unconscious forces and "fates", which include madness and death in their repertoire:-

"The secret is that only that which can destroy itself is truly alive. It is well that these things are difficult to understand and thus enjoy a wholesome concealment, for weak heads are only too easily addled by them and thrown into confusion." (CW14: *Mysterium Coniunctionis* - Pages 73/74 Para 93)

Unfortunately it is intemperate language of this nature which encourages us to identify our conscious attitudes with the archetypal and collective contents of the unconscious, in the revelationary promise of secrets and mysteries which are open only to initiates and individuants.

II

Perhaps the most celebrated artist who occupied himself with such themes was Leonardo da Vinci, in whose work the principle of androgyne achieves its highest expression. Ambivalence and ambiguity pervade much of his small output of paintings, and this can be seen in his development of the sfumato technique for the rendering of facial expression and in his use of conflicting perspectives in the background landscape of the *Mona Lisa*, where to the left and right of the sitter two irreconcilable views converge upon her. It can also be seen in the two different viewpoints which have been taken in the construction of the *Mona Lisa*'s face, and if there is a suggestion of androgyny about it, this may well be due to the possibility that it is not only the product of two viewpoints, but that of a fusion of two models; one male and one female. When one becomes aware of this disparity and tension between the opposites and their fusion within the figure of the *Mona Lisa*, one realises why the painting is so unsettling psychologically and how Leonardo has provided us with his own answer to the enigma.

One interesting illustration of such themes is provided by the *Trinity Altarpiece* in the National Gallery of Scotland, which is by the Flemish artist Hugo Van der Goes. This altarpiece demonstrates the complexity of 15th century religious symbolism and the extent to which the principles considered in Leonardo's work, which admittedly border on the secular, are pursued in relation to the Christian symbols. Nevertheless, in Hugo's work we discover a greatly different sensibility; one which comes across particularly clearly if we contrast Hugo's Trinity with that of Masaccio.

Christ is no longer the static image of the Cross that we see in Masaccio's version of the Trinity, but is held in his Father's arms, adopting the pose we see in many representations of the Deposition. His body is twisted and broken, and the emphasis is upon the suffering endured. All extraneous features have been removed from the composition and instead of setting the figures in an architectural space, Hugo chooses to place them on a golden throne within the indeterminate space of Heaven. Given the intense realism and the empirical perspective used by the artists of the Burgundian renaissance, some have argued that Hugo has used deliberately archaising features in this painting. The distortion of the throne, with its sweeping lines which encompass the figures is taken as an instance of this. However, the overall impact of the composition, with its spiral form and asymmetry provides us with a very direct and visionary experience of the Trinity and suggests that we are witnesses to a personal revelation. The very human quality of the figures indicates this, for like the figures of Masaccio they have been taken from life, but on this occasion there is no generational divide between the Son and Father. The directness of the scene is also highlighted by the fact that here the Father returns our gaze.

This background prepares us, therefore, for a consideration of the most problematical aspect of the Trinity panel, for into the composition Hugo introduces a fourth element which somewhat jars with the traditional schema of Father, Son and hovering Holy Spirit. This is the crystal orb at Christ's feet, which is described in the following way in the principal monograph on the painting, by Colin Thompson and Lorne Campbell:-

"The crystal orb of the world rolls away unheeded to one side." (Thompson)
"The crystal sphere at Christ's feet symbolises the world." (Campbell)
(*Hugo Van der Goes and the Trinity Panels in Edinburgh*)

As a symbol, the sphere has a wide range of meanings, but in considering them we should perhaps remember the specific way in which Renaissance artists used symbols in their paintings and remain cautious of applying this range of possible meanings all at once in a kind of generalised synthesis. However, a common denominator of this range is provided by the theme of perfection and perfectibility. The globe is used as a symbol of the gold at the end of the alchemical process. It is associated with the soul, the Platonic anima mundi, and with the original man, or unus mundus, the hermaphrodite in which the sexes are fused or are as yet unseparated. It is a symbol of the corpus rotundum of alchemy, which expresses the range of stages in the transformation process. The orb is a symbol of kingship and of magistery and is often shown with the markings of a "T" within its circumference. The earliest maps we have of the world are known as "T.O." maps, because the crude arrangement of the then known continents, Asia, Africa and Europe, form a "T" within a flat disk. In some paintings of the Assumption of the Virgin and the Ascension of Christ the divine figure is contained within a circular disk on its ascent to heaven. In altarpieces which illustrate the Last Judgement, Christ is often shown standing upon an orb, and in representations of visions of God the Father both orb and disk feature, thus indicating that the symbol also has a teleological aspect. And finally, in Jung's psychology the sphere as a mandala is a symbol of the self.

This is not to say that such preoccupations are a feature of the work of the majority of artists of the time, but there is a tradition strong enough to warrant special study and consideration. In this respect, one of the most interesting themes of the art of the 15th century is that of the visions of the great mystic saints: Anthony Abbot, George, Eustace, Jerome and John of Patmos. In a small predella panel in the National Gallery, which shows St. John the Baptist retiring to the desert, Giovanni di Paulo illustrates some of the features which are common to paintings of this type. The saint sets out on his journey or peregrination into the wilderness, leaving behind him the ordered world of the city or the field in favour of the fantastic forms of nature.

The landscapes shown in these paintings abound with bizarre twisted rock formations or soaring mountains, and the landscapes themselves form a part of a hallucinatory vision which indicates we are in the territory not only of nature, but of an objective psyche which has the ability to reveal to us such visions. Giovanni adds a telling comment on this in the form of the exquisitely rendered borders which indicate a white rose at the left and a reddish one at the right. The colours refer to two stages in the alchemical process; the albedo or whitening which follows black despair of the nigredo, and the rubedo, the reddening which precedes the production of the philosophical stone, which in this context relates to the experience of the great vision or enlightenment of the saint. Other artists concentrated more upon the gruesome horrors in their visions of hell and torment. The Temptation of St. Anthony by Hieronymus Bosch is well known, but even Giorgione linked these themes in his Landscape with St. Roche, St. George and St. Anthony Abbot, by showing a couple of ungainly monsters in the foreground of an otherwise idyllic scene. The subject of St. George and the dragon shows most clearly the understanding of the link between these monstrous apparitions and the final stage, for to the saint is revealed a vision of the darker side of creation: its shadow.

III

One common denominator of all of Hugo's extant religious works is the way in which each one of them places ordinary, realistically observed and even humble, human beings in the context of the great mysteries and events of the Christian faith. Considering the fact that Hugo himself became a monk we may have further grounds for feeling that he was not simply giving expression to the philosophical mood of the Christianity of the Netherlands and Burgundy, but also to a deep personal experience. This much is suggested by the unprecedentedly original use of the symbol of the crystal orb in the Trinity altarpiece. But from Lorne Campbell's summary of Hugo's biography we learn the following:-

"Five or six years after he had taken his vows, Hugo went to Cologne. On his return journey, he was afflicted with madness, believing himself damned and attempting to injure himself. Brought to Brussels, and then back to the Rode Klooster, he recovered, apparently only to die shortly afterwards." (*Hugo Van der Goes & the Trinity Panels in Edinburgh.*)

The bald outlines of the story indicate that Hugo succumbed to what we would now refer to as a psychosis and that this was closely connected with his religious outlook; that his hubris of placing man so near the centre stage of the divine drama led to an enantiodromia which found its expression in the fear of being damned and in the dramatic reaction of self-mutilation. Nevertheless, Hugo's Trinity reflects a general mood which we find in 15th century religious paintings which reveal an anticipation of a fresh or renewed revelation. Indeed this takes the form of a fresh visitation of God upon man, as God chooses to announce himself, thus re-emphasising man's closeness to him. However, if we recall the symbolic content of myths which concern man's closeness to this drama, there is always the danger that we identify with the divine figures, appropriating to us their powers and suffering as a consequence the fates of Prometheus, Sisyphus, Marsyas or Actaeon. In the absence of a sense of perspective, of man's true position within such a cosmic scheme of things, we find that "the centre cannot hold"; that the creative tension which yields to us a momentary release from the conditions and conflicts of the opposites can lead to a fission and splitting apart which intensifies them and can be expressed as imbalance and psychosis.

Appendix
Revised versions of two poems

The Magic Mountain

I am not to be deceived
    by the albino maiden
Who gave me her ring
    in the knowledge of forms
    as yet unformed
    of nameless upwelling impulses

I am not to be deceived
    by the dry sky
    over mountains
Nor by the stillness
    its empty peace

Romantic poets and artists sought out such scenery
Regarding the mountains as
    dwelling places of the spirit
Fixing ascendency to their peaks
Yearning to their uprising thrust

For the mountain has its awesome aspect
Communing with the material belly of earth
Rending down to twisted folds
    of ravines and rockfalls
Where sudden movements spell danger
Where heroic gestures presage fall

Our hubris mocks shadowy places
Naming as myth the Elysian Fields and River Styx
 the boatman and his accompanying hands
Would such ignorance have the face to laugh
 in these matters?
Would it prove to be any preparation?

The corn tremors in the wind
Colours pulsate the fullness of flowers
 in the meadow
Red bathes the river with the last
 of many dying suns

The Voyage into Night

I came into this world as if in a dream
Hallucinating to the stars in the night
Dark visions of Our Lady
Holding the torch
It was frightening
To sense one's progression so
Voyaging into Night

In the dark
It is peopled by the merry-go-round kaleidoscope
Round and round go the vistas
Unfolding
A strange entertainment
To retire to between the sheets

One night came a twist
I was unreachable
Journeying alone
Sentient creature
Caught between good and evil
Their faces
Mocking my loneliness

The jerk into it
Comes suddenly
Think pleasant thoughts
Abate this restlessness

Dying is in the wrong tense
With it comes an unfolding
Too easy and too gentle
When there is no unfolding
Only it is the whiplash

I cannot recall it
Distanced as I am
Caught up in the act of living
The only unfolding